AI in UX Design

How UX Designers are Using AI in the Age of Artificial Intelligence

Updated & Expanded Edition

This book is provided for informational and educational purposes only. The author makes no guarantees regarding the accuracy or completeness of the content and is not responsible for how the information is used.

Note: AI software was used to create illustrations for this book.

Table of Contents

Preface

When my first book, *AI for UX Designers,* was first published, artificial intelligence was already beginning to influence how digital products were designed. Designers were experimenting with AI-powered features, recommendation systems, and early automation tools. The conversation was important but still emerging.

Since then, everything has changed.

Generative AI has moved from the margins to the center of product design. Tools powered by large language models are now part of everyday workflows. Designers are no longer just designing for AI-powered systems; they are designing with them. AI has become a thinking partner, a research assistant, a prototyping accelerator, and, increasingly, a builder.

The original edition of this book focused on helping UX designers understand AI concepts and design responsibly for intelligent systems. This updated edition exists because the role of the UX designer has fundamentally shifted.

Today, designers are framing problems alongside AI, synthesizing research with AI assistance, generating personas, journeys, and requirements faster than ever, prototyping earlier, sometimes before wireframes even exist, validating ideas with real users in days instead of months, and in some cases shipping real software without traditional development handoffs.

This is not a minor evolution of UX practice. It is a structural change in how products are conceived, designed, validated, and built.

This book is not an incremental refresh. It is a reorientation.

The rise of generative AI, no-code tooling, and AI-assisted software development has collapsed traditional boundaries between design, product, and engineering. The familiar linear process—research, wireframes, prototypes, handoff—is being replaced by a more fluid, iterative, and accelerated model where prototypes are created earlier, and learning happens continuously.

Designers who understand this shift are moving faster, taking on more ownership, and shaping products more directly. Designers who don't risk being left behind, not because they lack talent, but because the tools and expectations around them have changed.

This edition exists to reflect how UX work is happening now.

This book is written for practicing UX designers, product designers, and design leaders who want to stay relevant in a generative AI world.

It is practical, not theoretical. It is tool-aware, but not tool-obsessed. It is grounded in real workflows, not hype. It is focused on outcomes, not novelty.

It is not a machine learning textbook. It does not require you to write code. It does not assume you want to become an engineer.

Instead, it assumes something more important: that designers are uniquely positioned to orchestrate AI-powered systems because they understand human needs, context, behavior, and experience.

With modern AI tools at our fingertips, the designer's role is expanding.

Designers are becoming experience orchestrators, early-stage builders, product thinkers, and increasingly, entrepreneurs.

When a prototype can be generated, tested, refined, and turned into working software with AI-assisted development tools, the designer is no longer waiting for permission to build. The designer is leading.

This book exists to help you do exactly that, responsibly, thoughtfully, and with humans at the center.

You don't need to read this book cover to cover in one sitting. Many chapters are designed to be referenced as you work. The case study is intentionally visual and process-driven, showing how AI can be woven through the entire UX lifecycle—from idea to validated prototype to deployable product.

If you are new to AI in UX, this book will get you up to speed quickly. If you are already experimenting, it will help you refine your process and think more strategically. If you are leading teams, it will help you understand how expectations and opportunities are changing.

The future of UX design is not about replacing human judgment with artificial intelligence. It is about amplifying human insight with powerful tools.

This edition exists because that future is no longer theoretical. It's already here.

Who This Book Is For

This book is written for UX designers who sense that their role is changing, and want to stay ahead of that change rather than react to it later.

It is for practicing UX designers, product designers, and design leaders who are curious about generative AI, already experimenting with it, or feeling pressure to understand how it is reshaping their work. It is especially relevant for designers working in digital products, SaaS, platforms, and consumer applications where AI is becoming embedded into everyday user experiences.

This book is for you if you want to:

- Design better products faster without sacrificing human-centered principles.
- Use generative AI as a thinking partner, not a shortcut.
- Accelerate discovery, synthesis, and prototyping responsibly.
- Prototype earlier and validate ideas sooner with real users.
- Understand how AI changes the UX process—not just the tools.
- Expand your role beyond execution into product thinking and orchestration.
- Explore how designers can move closer to entrepreneurship and ownership.

You do not need to be an AI expert to read this book. You do not need a technical background. You do not need to write code.

You do need a solid foundation in UX design, product design, or a closely related discipline. This book assumes you understand core concepts like user research, usability, interaction design, and iterative design, even if your organization practices them imperfectly.

This book is also written with senior designers and design leaders in mind. If you are responsible for defining UX strategy, evolving design processes, mentoring others, or influencing product direction, you'll find frameworks and examples that help you navigate how AI is reshaping expectations across teams.

At the same time, this book is intentionally not for everyone.

It is not a beginner's guide to UX design. If you are brand new to UX, you may find some sections move quickly or assume familiarity with standard design practices.

It is not a technical manual for machine learning or artificial intelligence. You will not find equations, model architectures, or deep dives into how AI systems are trained.

It is not a step-by-step coding book. While it discusses AI-assisted software development and no-code tools, the focus is on how designers guide and orchestrate these systems—not how to become a full-stack engineer.

And it is not a book about replacing designers with AI.

This book takes a clear stance: the value of UX designers increases when AI is used well. Designers who understand how to frame problems, guide AI tools, validate outcomes with real humans, and orchestrate systems responsibly will be more influential, not less.

If you are looking for hype, shortcuts, or promises that AI will do your job for you, this book will likely disappoint you.

If you are looking for practical ways to design better products, move faster with confidence, and evolve your role in a generative AI world, you are exactly who this book was written for.

Chapter 1 – From UX Tools to AI Teammates

For most of the history of UX design, our tools have been static. They helped us document ideas, visualize interfaces, and simulate interactions, but they did not participate in thinking. Sketching tools captured concepts. Wireframing tools organized structure. Prototyping tools demonstrated flow. Research tools stored findings. No matter how advanced the software became, the cognitive work remained firmly with the designer.

That relationship has fundamentally changed.

Generative AI introduces a new class of tools that do not simply execute instructions, but actively contribute to the design process. These systems can analyze information, synthesize patterns, generate alternatives, and respond to context over time. Instead of acting as passive instruments, they behave more like collaborators.

This marks a shift from UX tools to UX teammates.

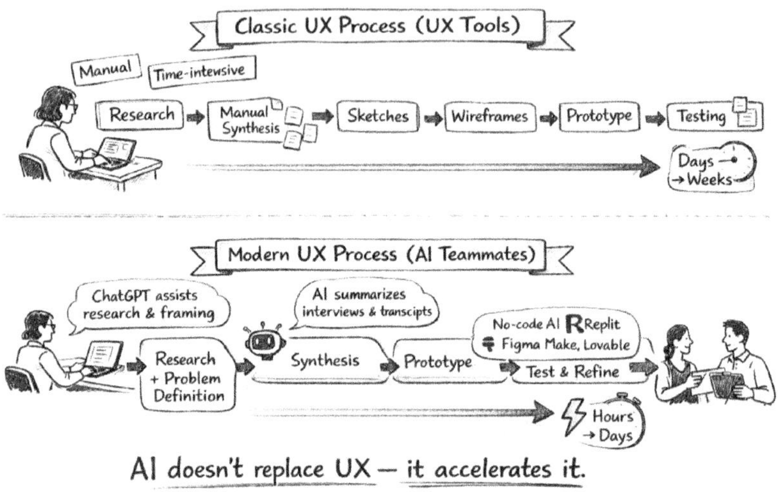

Designers are no longer working alone with software that waits for direction. They are working in dialogue with systems that can propose, critique, reframe, and expand ideas. This does not mean AI replaces design thinking. It means design thinking now happens in conversation rather than isolation.

This shift breaks many of the assumptions traditional UX processes were built on.

Classic UX workflows assumed that thinking was slow and making was expensive. Designers were expected to carefully analyze problems, document insights, and move deliberately toward solutions because creating and testing experiences required time and coordination. As a result, much of the design process focused on producing artifacts that represented intent rather than testing intent directly.

AI disrupts this model by collapsing the distance between thought and execution.

When ideas can be externalized quickly into interactive forms, designers no longer need to rely solely on abstract reasoning or static documentation. They can explore possibilities, challenge assumptions, and test behavior earlier and more frequently. Prototypes become a way to think, not just a way to validate.

This changes where risk lives in the process. Instead of being discovered late, uncertainty can be surfaced early. Instead of defending decisions through documentation, designers can learn through interaction.

Yet despite these changes, some things remain constant.

Human-centered design still matters.

AI does not understand users. It does not experience frustration, confusion, trust, or delight. It predicts language and patterns based on prior data, not lived experience. The responsibility for understanding human needs, context, and consequences still belongs to designers.

Empathy, judgment, and ethical responsibility do not become less important in an AI-driven world. They become more important.

As AI systems grow more capable, the cost of poor design decisions increases. Mistakes scale faster. Bias travels further. Overconfidence becomes more dangerous. Designers must remain grounded in research, validation, and critical thinking to ensure that speed does not replace understanding.

What has changed is what is expected of UX designers.

Designers are no longer valued solely for their ability to produce artifacts. They are increasingly valued for their ability to frame problems, guide exploration, and make sound decisions amid ambiguity. They are expected to work earlier in the product lifecycle, closer to strategy, and more collaboratively across disciplines.

They are also expected to orchestrate AI tools effectively.

This means knowing when to lean on AI and when to slow down. It means using AI to explore, not to decide. It means treating outputs as hypotheses rather than answers. And it means remaining accountable for outcomes, even when execution is automated.

In this new reality, the designer's role expands.

Designers become sense-makers, facilitators, and orchestrators of intelligent systems. They define intent, provide context, validate outcomes with real humans, and guide AI toward responsible solutions. They are not replaced by AI; they are amplified by it.

This chapter establishes the foundation for everything that follows.

The rest of this book explores how UX designers can work effectively with AI teammates, how to understand them, how to use them responsibly, and how to lead in a world where design is no longer just about making interfaces, but about shaping intelligent experiences.

Chapter 2 – The New Role of the UX Designer

For much of the past two decades, the role of the UX designer has been defined by craft. Designers were valued for their ability to translate abstract requirements into usable interfaces, create clear interaction patterns, and advocate for users within complex organizations. Success was often measured by the quality of deliverables: wireframes, prototypes, specifications, and polished designs.

That definition no longer captures the full scope of the role.

As generative AI becomes embedded in design and product workflows, the value of UX designers is shifting away from output and toward intent. What matters most is no longer how quickly a designer can produce artifacts, but how effectively they can define the right problem, guide exploration, and make sound decisions in the face of uncertainty.

This shift is subtle, but profound.

AI can now generate screens, flows, copy, and even interactive prototypes at speeds that would have been unthinkable just a few years ago. When production becomes abundant, judgment becomes scarce. And judgment is where experienced designers excel.

The modern UX designer is no longer just a maker of things. They are an orchestrator.

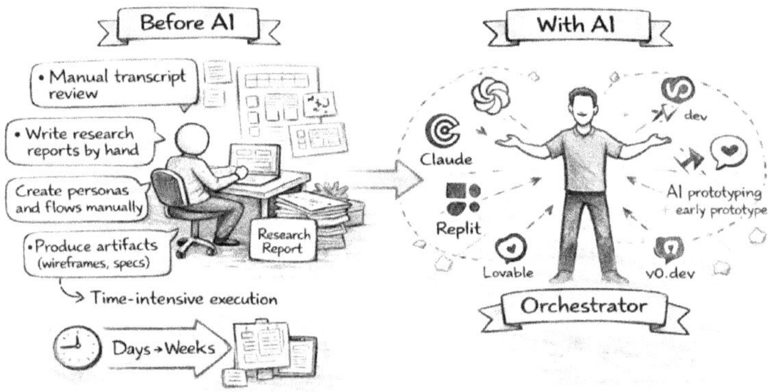

From manual execution to orchestration.

AI doesn't replace the UX Designer — it changes the leverage.

They bring clarity to ambiguity. They connect business goals to human needs. They recognize when a solution looks compelling but fails to address the real problem. They know when to trust AI-generated suggestions and when to question them.

In an AI-enabled environment, this ability becomes the designer's primary value.

As the mechanics of design accelerate, ownership moves upstream. Designers are increasingly involved earlier in the product lifecycle, shaping not just how something works, but why it exists in the first place.

They are expected to participate in problem definition, opportunity framing, and strategic decision-making, often alongside product managers, engineers, and business stakeholders.

In many cases, designers are now doing this work directly with AI tools as collaborators.

Instead of starting with a blank canvas, designers start with conversations. They explore multiple framings of a problem. They test assumptions quickly. They generate alternative paths and evaluate tradeoffs earlier. This changes the rhythm of design work from linear to iterative and conversational.

The designer's role becomes less about execution and more about orchestration.

Orchestration does not mean stepping away from craft. It means applying craft where it matters most. Designers still make critical decisions about interaction, flow, hierarchy, and tone. But they are no longer constrained by the speed of manual production. They can spend more time evaluating, refining, and validating ideas rather than producing them from scratch.

This shift also changes how designers collaborate with others.

When AI can scaffold prototypes and even generate working code, the traditional handoff between design and development becomes less rigid. Designers are no longer simply preparing artifacts for downstream teams. They are creating living representations of intent that can evolve directly into products.

This does not eliminate the need for engineers or product managers. But it does change the balance of responsibility. Designers who understand how to guide AI systems can take on more ownership earlier, reducing friction and misalignment later.

As a result, many designers are finding themselves closer to entrepreneurship than ever before.

With the ability to ideate, prototype, validate, and build without large teams, designers can move from concept to product faster and with less overhead. This opens new possibilities not just for startups, but for internal innovation, side projects, and new forms of leadership within organizations.

The designer becomes a catalyst.

This expanded role also carries greater responsibility.

AI systems are confident, persuasive, and sometimes wrong. They reflect the data they were trained on, and the assumptions embedded in their prompts. Designers must remain accountable for outcomes, ensuring that experiences are inclusive, ethical, and grounded in real user needs.

Human-centered design does not disappear in an AI-driven world. It becomes more important.

The new role of the UX designer is not to compete with AI, nor to surrender decision-making to it. It is to guide it. To shape its outputs with context, constraints, and care. To ensure that speed does not come at the expense of understanding.

This book is written for designers who are ready to step into that role.

Designers who are willing to move beyond execution, embrace ambiguity, and take ownership of the full arc of product creation. Designers who see AI not as a threat to their craft, but as a force that amplifies what they do best.

In the chapters that follow, we will move from this role shift into the practical realities of working with generative AI. You will learn how these tools work at a level that matters for design, how they fit into discovery and research, how they enable earlier prototyping, and how validated ideas can move more quickly into real products.

The tools will continue to evolve. Titles will change. Platforms will rise and fall.

But the role of the UX designer as a thoughtful, human-centered orchestrator of intelligent systems, is only becoming more essential.

Chapter 3 – Generative AI Explained

Generative AI has quickly become part of the everyday language of product teams, but much of the conversation around it is framed through a technical lens. Terms like models, parameters, tokens, and training data dominate explanations, leaving many designers either overwhelmed or disengaged.

That level of detail is rarely what UX designers need.

To work effectively with generative AI, designers don't need to understand how models are built. They need to understand how these systems behave, where they add value in the design process, and where they can mislead if used uncritically.

This chapter establishes a practical mental model for generative AI that is grounded in how designers think and work.

Generative AI, in UX terms, is a system that can take context, intent, and constraints and produce plausible outputs in response. Those outputs might be text, ideas, summaries, structures, flows, or even interface concepts. What makes these systems different from traditional software is that they do not follow fixed rules.

They generate responses based on patterns learned from vast amounts of data.

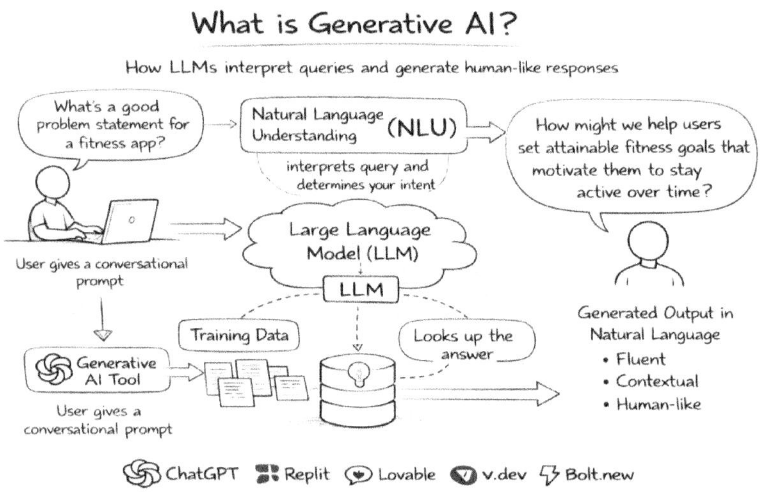

For designers, the most important shift is this: generative AI does not retrieve answers. It generates possibilities.

That distinction matters.

When you ask a generative AI system a question, it is not looking up a correct response in a database. It is predicting what a reasonable response might look like based on the context you provided. This makes generative AI especially powerful for early-stage design work, where exploration, framing, and synthesis matter more than precision.

It also makes it dangerous when treated as an authority.

Large language models, which power most generative AI tools used by designers, can be thought of as reasoning systems. They are not reasoning in a human sense, but they can follow logic, maintaining context, and responding coherently across a conversation. They can compare options, explain tradeoffs, reframe problems, and build on previous inputs.

For UX designers, this enables a new kind of interaction with tools.

Instead of issuing commands, designers engage in dialogue. They can refine a problem statement through multiple iterations. They can ask a system to challenge assumptions, explore edge cases, or view a situation from the perspective of different users. The quality of output depends less on a single perfect prompt and more on the designer's ability to guide the conversation over time.

This makes working with generative AI feel closer to collaborating with a junior teammate than operating a piece of software.

One of the greatest strengths designers can leverage is speed of exploration. Generative AI allows designers to move quickly through divergent thinking, generating multiple options, perspectives, and framings in minutes rather than days. This is especially valuable early in the design process when teams are still trying to understand the problem space.

Another strength is synthesis. Designers often work with messy, incomplete, or contradictory inputs, research notes, stakeholder opinions, business constraints, and user feedback. Generative AI can help summarize, organize, and surface patterns across this information, giving designers a clearer starting point for decision-making.

Generative AI also excels at articulation. It can help designers draft problem statements, personas, journey descriptions, and UX requirements that are clear and structured. This doesn't replace the designer's thinking, but it can reduce the friction of turning insights into communicable artifacts.

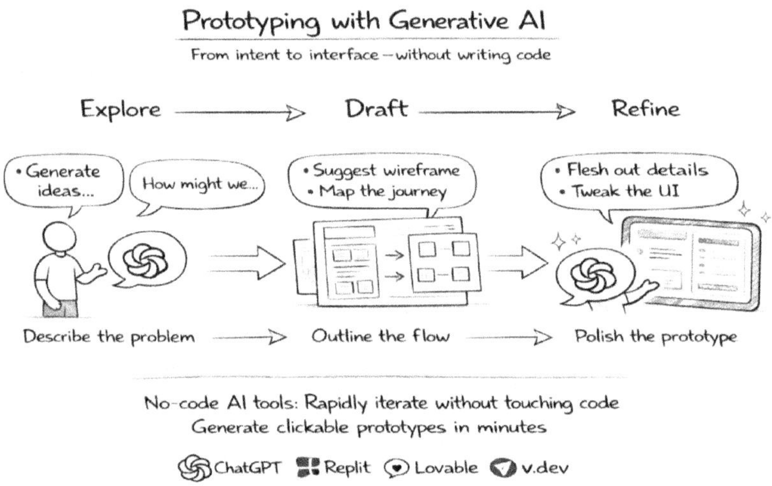

Perhaps most importantly, generative AI can act as a cognitive mirror. By responding to prompts, it reflects assumptions, gaps, and inconsistencies in how a problem is framed. Designers who pay attention to this feedback can sharpen their own thinking.

However, these strengths come with important limitations.

Generative AI systems are confident by default. They produce responses that sound plausible, polished, and authoritative, even when they are incomplete, biased, or wrong. They do not have awareness of truth, only patterns. This makes them especially risky when designers mistake fluency for accuracy.

These systems are also highly sensitive to context. Small changes in how a problem is framed can lead to very different outputs. If the input is vague, biased, or incomplete, the output will reflect that. Generative AI does not correct poor framing, it amplifies it.

Another limitation is that generative AI has no direct access to your users. It does not observe behavior, conduct interviews, or experience frustration. It can simulate perspectives based on patterns, but those simulations are approximations, not evidence. Designers must be careful not to confuse generated personas or insights with real user understanding.

There is also the risk of false confidence. Because generative AI can produce complete-looking outputs quickly, teams may feel pressure to move forward before ideas have been properly validated. Speed can mask uncertainty rather than resolve it.

For these reasons, AI output should always be treated as hypotheses, not truth.

A hypothesis is a starting point. It is something to test, refine, and validate. Generative AI is exceptionally good at helping designers generate hypotheses at scale. It is not good at confirming them.

The designer's role is to decide which hypotheses are worth pursuing and how they should be tested with real humans. This is where traditional UX skills such as research, usability testing, critical thinking, and empathy remain essential.

When used well, generative AI accelerates learning. When used poorly, it accelerates mistakes.

The goal of this book is not to teach you how to get better answers from AI. It is to help you ask better questions, frame better problems, and make better decisions with AI as a partner rather than an authority.

In the next chapter, we'll look at the specific generative AI tools UX designers are using today and how designers are applying them across the design process in practical, responsible ways.

Chapter 4 – The AI Tools UX Designers Use

As generative AI has entered mainstream use, dozens of tools and platforms have emerged. Some are deeply technical. Others are specialized for engineering, data science, or infrastructure. Most UX designers do not need to engage with that ecosystem directly.

In practice, most designers working with generative AI today rely on a small set of consumer-facing chat interfaces. These tools are accessible, flexible, and powerful enough to support discovery, synthesis, ideation, and early prototyping work without requiring technical setup.

This chapter focuses intentionally on those tools, not because they are the only options available, but because they are the ones designers are actually using.

The three tools most embedded in UX workflows today are **ChatGPT**, **Claude**, and **Gemini**. While they are built on similar underlying technologies, designers tend to use them in slightly different ways based on how they behave, respond, and fit into day-to-day work.

Understanding these differences helps designers choose the right tool for the right moment.

ChatGPT is often used as a general-purpose thinking partner. Designers turn to it for brainstorming, reframing problems, drafting artifacts, and exploring multiple directions quickly. It performs well when the goal is broad exploration or when a designer wants to move fluidly between topics within a single conversation.

Many designers use ChatGPT to generate first-pass problem statements, user scenarios, journey outlines, and UX requirements. It is especially useful when starting from ambiguity and needing momentum. Because of its versatility, it often becomes the default tool designers open first.

Claude is frequently used when clarity, structure, and longer reasoning matter. Designers often describe it as feeling more deliberate and reflective in its responses. This makes it particularly effective for synthesizing research, reviewing long documents, summarizing interviews, or stress-testing ideas.

When designers want to slow down, examine tradeoffs, or evaluate assumptions, Claude tends to be the tool of choice. It is commonly used to refine personas, analyze user needs, or critique early concepts rather than generate them from scratch.

Gemini is often used when designers are working close to existing information ecosystems, especially content that lives across documents, presentations, or collaborative environments. Designers use it to connect ideas, surface patterns, and integrate insights across sources.

No-Code AI Prototyping Tools

A growing class of no-code AI prototyping tools, including **Figma Make, Lovable, v0.dev, Bolt.new, Replit**, and **Base44**, allows designers to move from ideas to working software experiences far earlier in the design process. These platforms generate functional interfaces, interactions, and basic application logic from natural language prompts, design files, or simple specifications, without requiring traditional coding.

Rather than stopping at static wireframes or polished mockups, designers can create interactive prototypes that behave like real products. Screens respond to input, workflows execute, and core tasks can be completed end to end. This enables designers to test not only visual design, but business functionality and user flows with real people while concepts are still fluid.

By putting working experiences in front of users earlier, designers can validate whether they are solving the right problem and delivering an intuitive experience before development begins. Feedback becomes more concrete, assumptions surface faster, and teams align around observed behavior rather than interpretation. These tools shift prototyping from representation to experience, helping designers reduce risk and increase confidence in what gets built.

These distinctions are not rigid, and they will continue to evolve. What matters more than which tool you choose is how you use it.

Across all AI platforms, effective designers treat prompting as a UX skill.

Prompting is not about clever phrasing or secret commands. It is about clearly expressing intent, providing relevant context, and setting meaningful constraints. In many ways, prompting mirrors the same skills designers use when writing scenarios, crafting research questions, or defining requirements.

A good prompt frames a problem the way a good design brief does. It explains who the user is, what they are trying to accomplish, what constraints exist, and what success looks like. Poor prompts produce vague outputs for the same reason vague requirements produce weak designs.

Designers who get the most value from generative AI rarely rely on a single prompt. Instead, they work iteratively. They respond to outputs, refine context, ask follow-up questions, and progressively shape the conversation. The AI's response becomes input for the next step, not a final answer.

Context plays a critical role in this process. The more relevant context a designer provides about users, goals, constraints, or prior decisions, the more useful the output becomes. This is why conversations tend to produce better results than isolated prompts. Over time, the AI begins to reflect the designer's intent more accurately.

Iteration also helps surface flaws. When designers ask an AI system to explain its reasoning, compare alternatives, or challenge its own suggestions, weaknesses become visible.

This mirrors design critique, where ideas are strengthened through examination rather than accepted at face value.

Knowing when to trust AI output is just as important as knowing how to generate it.

Generative AI is well suited for exploration, synthesis, articulation, and pattern recognition. It is useful when designers are trying to understand a problem space, generate options, or communicate ideas more clearly.

It should be treated with caution when precision, factual accuracy, or deep contextual understanding is required. AI does not know your users, your business, or your constraints unless you explicitly provide that information, and even then, it can only approximate understanding.

Designers should be especially careful when AI outputs feel overly confident or complete. Polished language can mask shallow reasoning. Outputs that look finished may still be based on untested assumptions.

The safest posture is to assume that AI outputs are directionally useful but incomplete. They are a way to move thinking forward, not a substitute for validation.

Designers remain responsible for deciding what is true, what is ethical, and what is worth building.

Used thoughtfully, these tools can dramatically accelerate UX work. Used uncritically, they can create the illusion of progress without understanding.

In the next chapter, we'll move from tools to application, focusing on how designers use generative AI to define problems more clearly and uncover opportunities earlier in the design process.

AI Tools UX Designers Actually Use Across the Design Process

UX Phase	Core Activities	How Designers Use AI	Common Tools
Discovery & Research	Research planning, interviews, synthesis	Drafts research guides, auto-transcribes sessions, clusters themes, summarizes insights	**ChatGPT**, **Claude**, **Dovetail**
Problem Definition	Problem framing, scope, constraints	Rewrites problem statements, tests framing, surfaces assumptions	ChatGPT, Claude
Personas & Journeys	Personas, journey maps, friction points	Generates draft personas, maps stages, identifies emotional highs and lows	ChatGPT, Claude
Ideation & Concepting	Concept generation, exploration	Rapid brainstorming, idea expansion, scenario exploration	ChatGPT
Information Architecture	Navigation, hierarchy, labeling	Proposes IA structures, naming systems, logic checks	ChatGPT, Claude
Interaction & UX Writing	Microcopy, states, interactions	Generates copy variants, adjusts tone, flags ambiguity	ChatGPT
Prototyping (Low → High Fidelity)	Flows, screens, interactive prototypes	Converts prompts into UI, builds functional prototypes without full engineering	**Figma Make**, **Lovable**, **v0.dev**, **Bolt.new**, **Replit**, **Base44**
Critique & Iteration	Review, refinement, risk analysis	Challenges assumptions, compares alternatives, identifies gaps	Claude
Build & Engineering Handoff	From prototype to production	Generates and refines production code directly in the dev environment	**Claude Code**
Communication & Alignment	Presentations, rationale, decisions	Converts work into clear narratives and stakeholder-ready decks	**Gamma**, **Gemini**, ChatGPT

Chapter 5 – AI-Assisted Problem Definition

Many product teams do not struggle because they lack ideas.
They struggle because they are solving the wrong problem.

Before any interface is designed or any prototype is built, teams must align on what problem deserves attention. This has always been one of the most important, and most difficult, responsibilities of UX research and design.

Traditionally, problem definition has been slow, manual, and cognitively heavy work. Designers and researchers conduct interviews, moderate focus groups, review transcripts, tag notes, and assemble research reports to extract meaning from qualitative data. This process is valuable, but it is also time-intensive and exhausting. Weeks can pass before insights are synthesized clearly enough to inform design decisions.

Generative AI fundamentally changes this phase of the workflow.

Not by replacing research, but by removing the friction between research activity and design readiness.

From Raw Research to Design-Ready Insight

In a traditional research process, designers often face a familiar scene: dozens of interview transcripts, messy notes, overlapping observations, and partially formed insights scattered across documents, sticky notes, and slide decks. Making sense of this information requires intense focus and repeated passes over the data.

Generative AI can now assist directly with this synthesis work.

Researchers can input raw transcripts, focus group notes, survey responses, and observational summaries into an AI system and ask it to:

- Identify recurring themes and patterns.
- Cluster related behaviors and pain points.
- Surface contradictions or outliers.
- Summarize insights across participants.

What once required days of manual synthesis can now be reduced to hours, without losing rigor.

The key shift is that designers no longer start problem definition from chaos. They start from **structured signal**.

Turning Insights into Actionable Artifacts

Problem definition does not end with insights. Design teams need artifacts that translate understanding into action.

This is another area where AI meaningfully accelerates the process.

From synthesized research, designers can use AI to generate first-pass versions of core UX artifacts, including:

- **Problem statements** that clearly articulate user needs and constraints.
- **Personas** grounded in observed behaviors.
- **User needs statements** framed as testable hypotheses.
- **User requirements** aligned to real goals and frustrations.
- **Success criteria** that define what "good" looks like.

These outputs are not meant to be accepted blindly. They are drafts that serve as starting points that designers refine with judgment, context, and validation.

But they eliminate the blank-page problem.

Instead of spending days translating research into artifacts, designers can move directly into reviewing, refining, and testing them. This dramatically shortens the path from discovery to design.

AI as a Research Synthesis Partner

One of the most powerful uses of generative AI in problem definition is its role as a synthesis partner.

Designers can ask AI questions such as:

- "What unmet needs appear across these interviews?"

- "Which frustrations are mentioned most frequently?"
- "What assumptions are implied in these user statements?"
- "How would you summarize this research for a product team?"

AI does not decide which insights matter—but it helps surface them faster and more comprehensively than a single human can working alone.

This allows designers to focus on interpretation, not transcription.

From Overwhelm to Clarity

This shift is not just about speed. It fundamentally changes the cognitive experience of research and design.

Without AI, designers often feel overwhelmed early in the process, buried in notes, struggling to maintain mental models of complex user data, and pressured to produce clarity on tight timelines.

With AI assisting synthesis and artifact generation, the designer's role changes.

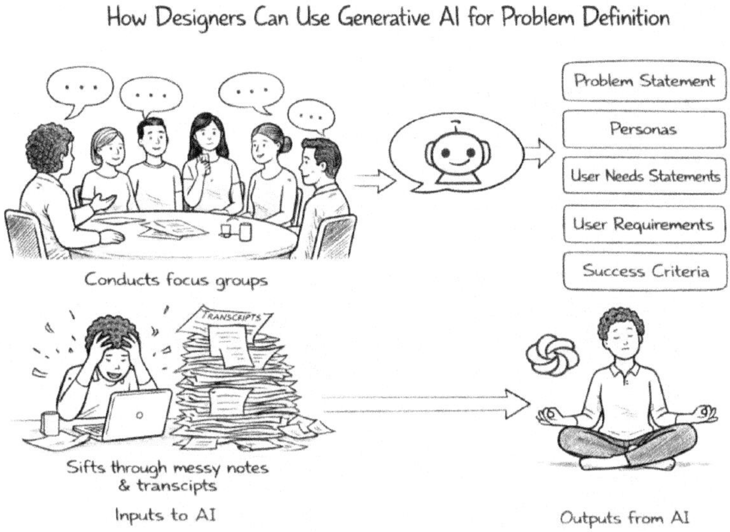

Instead of manually processing everything, the designer orchestrates the flow:

- Human research generates raw insight.
- AI organizes, synthesizes, and structures information.
- The designer evaluates, refines, and decides what moves forward.

This is the transition illustrated at the end of this chapter: from chaos to clarity, from overwhelm to focus.

The designer is no longer buried under research. They feel centered and able to think, reason, and move forward with confidence.

What AI Changes—and What It Doesn't

AI does not eliminate the need for user research.
It does not validate insights.
It does not understand nuance, emotion, or context the way humans do.

What it does is remove unnecessary friction. It shortens the distance between **learning** and **making**.

By the time designers move into prototyping, they are no longer guessing at the problem. They are working from a clear, structured understanding that is supported by research, articulated through usable artifacts, and ready to be tested.

Problem definition remains a human responsibility.
AI simply makes it easier to do well.

Why This Matters

When teams can define problems faster and more clearly, everything downstream improves:

- Prototypes are built earlier.
- Experiments happen sooner.
- Feedback loops tighten.
- Waste decreases.

The result is not just efficiency.
It is better alignment between what teams build and what users need.

In the next few chapters, we'll look at how designers use AI to move from problem definition into rapid prototyping, turning intent into interfaces faster than ever before.

Chapter 6 – Understanding Users with AI

Understanding users has always been at the heart of UX design. No amount of technology changes the fundamental truth that good products emerge from a deep understanding of human needs, behaviors, and constraints. What generative AI changes is not the importance of user understanding, but how designers prepare for, accelerate, and synthesize that understanding.

AI can help designers think more clearly about users earlier in the process, but it cannot replace real research. The distinction matters.

One of the most common and useful applications of AI in UX work is the creation of personas. Personas are not final representations of users. They are informed starting points, or working models that help designers articulate assumptions about who users might be and what they might care about.

Generative AI can help designers draft these early profiles quickly. By providing context about the product, domain, and target audience, designers can generate plausible user segments, goals, frustrations, and behaviors. This helps teams align early and creates a shared language for discussion.

However, these outputs must be treated carefully. AI-generated personas are not evidence. They are hypotheses. Their value lies in making assumptions visible so they can be tested, refined, or discarded through research.

Used responsibly, personas help designers move into research with clearer questions and sharper focus.

Beyond personas, AI can assist designers in articulating user needs, motivations, and constraints. Designers often work with incomplete or fragmented information early on. AI can help organize these fragments into coherent narratives that highlight what users are trying to achieve, what stands in their way, and what tradeoffs they are making.

This kind of synthesis is especially helpful when designers are working across complex systems or multiple user groups. AI can help surface patterns across roles, contexts, and behaviors, providing a structured lens through which to examine emerging insights.

Contextual understanding is another area where AI can support design thinking. Designers can use AI to explore how behavior might change across environments, time pressures, emotional states, or levels of expertise. This supports more nuanced framing of user journeys and helps teams avoid overly simplistic assumptions.

Again, these are explorations, not conclusions.

AI does not observe users in their environment. It does not experience friction, confusion, or delight. It simulates likely patterns based on what it has seen before. Designers must remain grounded in the reality that actual user behavior is often messier, more contradictory, and more revealing than any generated description.

One of the most powerful uses of AI in this stage is helping designers design better research.

By reflecting on proto-personas and early hypotheses, designers can ask AI to help identify gaps in understanding, suggest areas of uncertainty, or propose questions worth exploring. This can inform interview guides, survey questions, and usability testing scenarios.

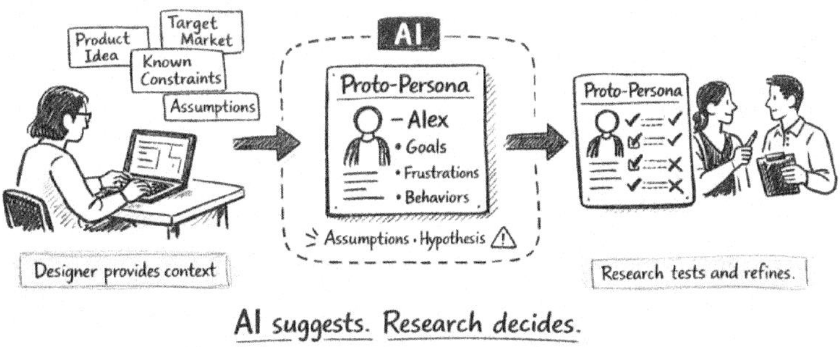

AI can also help designers think critically about bias. By asking an AI system to identify whose perspectives might be missing or which assumptions might reflect organizational bias rather than user reality, designers can design more inclusive and intentional research plans.

This shifts AI's role from replacing research to strengthening it.

Despite these benefits, there are clear boundaries that designers must respect.

AI cannot validate user needs.
AI cannot confirm motivations.
AI cannot observe behavior.
AI cannot feel frustration or delight.

Only real humans can do that.

Anything that directly informs product decisions, such as prioritization, requirements, and success criteria, must ultimately be grounded in evidence gathered from real users. AI can help designers prepare, synthesize, and reflect, but it cannot substitute for listening, observing, and learning.

Designers must be especially cautious when AI outputs feel emotionally resonant or intuitively correct. Plausible narratives are not proof. Empathy must be earned through engagement, not generated through language.

When designers use AI responsibly at this stage, they enter research better prepared and exit it with greater clarity. They ask sharper questions, recognize patterns sooner, and articulate insights more effectively.

The result is not less human-centered design, but more supported by tools that help designers focus their attention where it matters most.

In the next chapter, we'll look at how AI supports the transition from understanding users to defining what needs to be designed, focusing on jobs to be done, user flows, and UX requirements.

Chapter 7 – Jobs to Be Done, UX Flows, and Requirements

Once designers have framed the problem and developed an initial understanding of users, the next challenge is translating insight into action. This is where many teams struggle. Research findings are often rich but abstract, and the path from insight to design decisions can feel unclear.

Generative AI can help bridge this gap by supporting synthesis, structure, and clarity without taking ownership away from the designer.

One of the most effective frameworks for this stage is Jobs to Be Done. JTBD shifts the focus away from who users are and toward what they are trying to accomplish. It emphasizes progress over preference and behavior over demographics.

AI is particularly well suited to helping designers synthesize jobs to be done from messy inputs. By providing research notes, interview summaries, or proto-personas, designers can ask AI to identify recurring goals, struggles, and triggers. This can surface patterns that might otherwise take multiple rounds of manual synthesis.

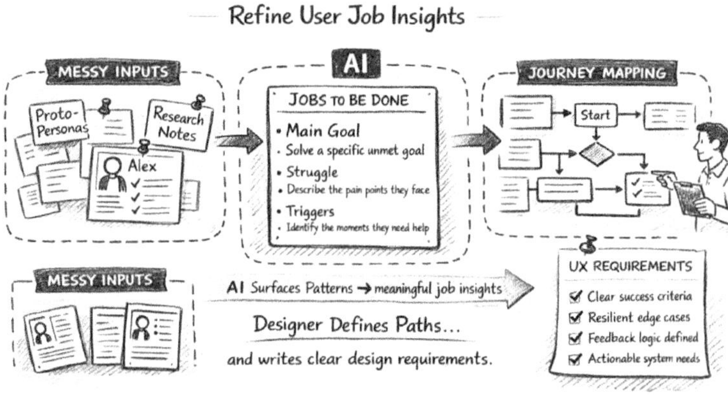

Importantly, AI should not be used to invent jobs. It should be used to organize and articulate what designers already suspect or have observed. The output becomes a draft set of jobs that designers can review, refine, and validate.

Effective JTBD work goes beyond functional outcomes. Users are not just trying to complete tasks; they are trying to feel a certain way or be perceived in a certain light. Emotional and social jobs often drive behavior more strongly than functional needs.

AI can help designers explore these dimensions by prompting reflection. Designers can ask how users might feel before, during, and after a job is completed, or how success might affect their confidence, reputation, or sense of control. These explorations can enrich understanding and prevent solutions from becoming overly mechanical.

As with all AI-assisted outputs, these interpretations are hypotheses. Emotional and social jobs must be validated through real conversations and observations. Still, AI can help ensure they are considered rather than overlooked.

Once jobs are defined, designers turn toward mapping journeys and flows. This is where understanding becomes structure.

AI can assist designers in outlining end-to-end journeys that connect user goals to system responses. Designers can explore how users enter an experience, what steps they take to make progress, and where friction or uncertainty may arise. This helps create a shared view of the experience before visual design begins.

These journey outlines are especially useful for identifying moments that matter, decision points, handoffs, and transitions where users are likely to struggle or disengage. AI can help surface these moments by analyzing flows for complexity, ambiguity, or dependency.

Designers must still apply judgment. AI can suggest paths, but it cannot decide which ones are appropriate for a given product, user, or context.

Another critical contribution of AI at this stage is identifying edge cases and failure states. Many UX issues arise not from the happy path, but from what happens when something goes wrong. Users enter unexpected inputs, misunderstand instructions, or encounter system limitations.

Designers can ask AI to stress-test flows by imagining what might happen when assumptions break. This can reveal gaps in logic, unclear feedback, or missing states that need to be designed intentionally.

Anticipating failure early leads to more resilient and humane experiences.

As flows and journeys become clearer, designers must translate insight into UX requirements. This is often where design intent is lost. Requirements can become vague, overly technical, or disconnected from user needs.

AI can help designers articulate requirements that are structured, traceable, and grounded in user goals. By tying requirements back to jobs and journeys, designers can ensure that each requirement serves a clear purpose.

For example, instead of stating that a system should "provide feedback," designers can specify what kind of feedback is needed, when it should appear, and how it should support user confidence or understanding. AI can help draft these descriptions, but designers must review them critically to ensure they reflect real needs rather than generic best practices.

Throughout this stage, the designer's role is not diminished by AI. It is clarified.

AI can help accelerate synthesis, surface patterns, and articulate structure. It cannot decide what matters, what is ethical, or what is appropriate for a specific group of users.

Those decisions remain human.

When used thoughtfully, AI helps designers move from insight to intent with greater clarity and less friction. It supports continuity across discovery, definition, and design, reducing the risk that important insights are lost along the way.

In the next chapter, we'll examine how these clarified flows and requirements enable a shift in the UX process itself, allowing designers to prototype earlier, validate sooner, and learn faster than traditional models allow.

Chapter 8 – Prototyping "shifts left" in the UX Process

For decades, UX design followed a familiar sequence. Teams researched, synthesized, sketched, wireframed, prototyped, and tested, often in that order. Prototyping was treated as a downstream activity, something that happened only after ideas had been carefully defined and refined.

That process made sense when creating prototypes was expensive and slow.

Today, that assumption no longer holds.

Generative AI and no-code tools have dramatically reduced the cost and effort required to create interactive experiences. As a result, the role of prototyping has changed. Prototyping is no longer a late-stage validation step. It has moved earlier in the process, sometimes becoming the first tangible expression of an idea.

This shift is often described as "shift-left" prototyping, but the term understates the impact. What's really changing is how designers think.

The classic UX process was built around sequential certainty. Each phase was expected to reduce risk before moving to the next. Research was meant to clarify the problem. Wireframes were meant to clarify structure. Prototypes were meant to validate decisions that had already been made.

In practice, this often led to false confidence. Teams invested heavily in documentation and static artifacts before testing assumptions in the real world. By the time prototypes reached users, key decisions were already locked in, making change difficult and expensive.

AI changes this dynamic by making it easier to externalize thinking early.

When designers can generate interactive representations quickly, they don't need to wait for perfect clarity before testing ideas. Prototypes become a way to explore uncertainty rather than confirm decisions. They allow designers to learn by making, rather than speculate through documentation.

AI-enabled prototyping allows designers to move directly from problem framing to tangible experiences. Instead of debating abstract concepts, teams can react to something concrete. This accelerates understanding not just for designers, but for stakeholders and users as well.

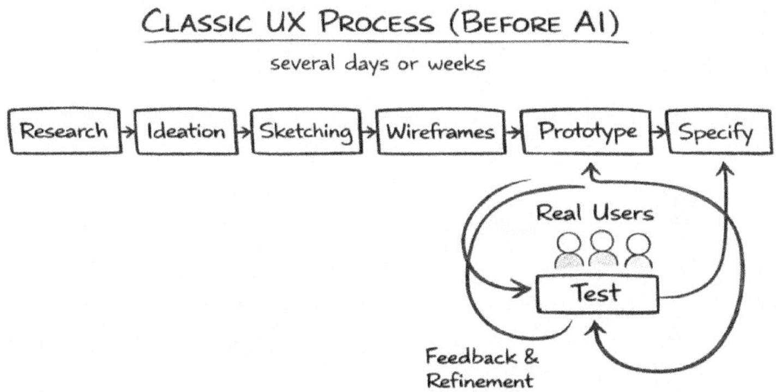

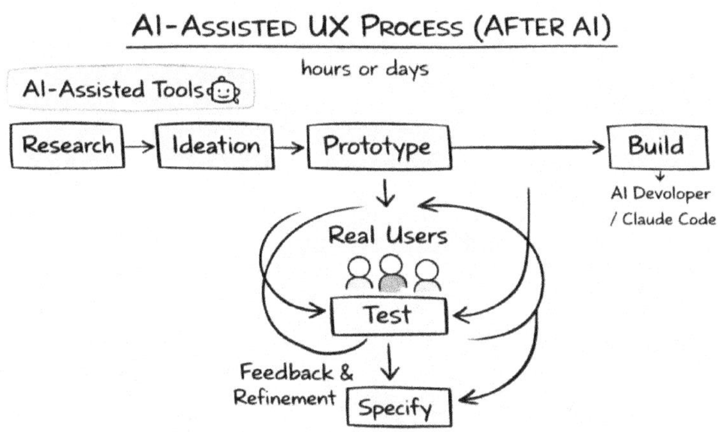

In this model, prototypes are not just representations of solutions. They are thinking tools.

By interacting with a prototype, designers can uncover gaps in logic, mismatches in expectations, and unanticipated user behaviors. These insights often emerge faster and more clearly than they would through discussion alone.

Prototypes also serve as powerful validation tools. When users interact with something that behaves like a real product, feedback becomes more grounded. Users respond to what they experience, not what they imagine. This leads to more actionable insights and fewer misunderstandings.

AI makes this possible earlier by reducing the friction of creation. Designers can generate flows, logic, and interactions without waiting on engineering or spending weeks refining fidelity. This does not mean quality is sacrificed. It means quality is tested sooner.

Earlier prototyping leads to faster feedback loops.

Instead of waiting weeks or months between learning cycles, designers can iterate in days. Each prototype informs the next, gradually increasing confidence while keeping options open. This rhythm supports learning over perfection.

Faster feedback also reduces rework. When assumptions are tested early, teams avoid building features that don't resonate with users. Problems surface before they are deeply embedded in architecture or code. This saves time, money, and morale.

From a business perspective, this shift has a direct impact on time to market. Products move from idea to validated concept more quickly. Teams gain confidence earlier. Decisions are informed by evidence rather than opinion.

Importantly, the ability to generate rapid prototypes earlier does not eliminate earlier UX practices. Research, synthesis, and framing still matter. What changes is how tightly they are coupled to making and testing.

Designers move fluidly between understanding and creating. They explore, test, reflect, and refine in short cycles rather than long phases. AI supports this flow by handling much of the mechanical work, freeing designers to focus on judgment and intent.

This shift also changes collaboration. When prototypes appear earlier, conversations become more productive. Stakeholders can respond to real interactions rather than abstract descriptions. Engineers can engage sooner, seeing how experiences are meant to behave rather than interpreting static artifacts.

The result is alignment through experience, not documentation.

AI prototyping is not about moving faster for its own sake. It is about learning sooner, reducing risk earlier, and making better decisions with less waste.

In the next chapter, we'll look at the tools that make this shift possible and how UX designers are using no-code and AI-assisted platforms to prototype earlier, iterate faster, and validate ideas with confidence.

Chapter 9 – No-Code AI Prototyping for UX Designers

For most of the history of UX design, prototyping required tradeoffs. Designers had to choose between speed and realism, between fidelity and flexibility. Building something interactive early often meant involving engineering, learning new tools, or accepting rough approximations of how a product would behave.

That constraint has largely disappeared.

No-code and AI-assisted prototyping tools now allow designers to create interactive, logic-driven experiences earlier than ever before. What once required weeks of setup or cross-functional coordination can now be explored in hours or days. As a result, designers no longer need to wait until ideas are fully formed to begin prototyping.

This is why designers can prototype earlier, not because the UX process has changed in theory, but because the cost of making has dropped dramatically.

When creation becomes easier, experimentation becomes safer.

Modern no-code tools allow designers to move directly from intent to interaction. Instead of documenting how something should work, designers can show it. Instead of debating edge cases abstractly, they can simulate them. This makes prototyping a core part of discovery and definition, not just validation.

Several tools have emerged as especially useful in this new workflow.

Figma remains central to many designers' workflows, but its role has expanded. Beyond static design and interaction prototyping, designers increasingly use it to explore flows, system states, and transitions earlier. With AI-assisted features and integrations, Figma becomes a space not just for design output, but for collaborative thinking.

Replit enables designers to move beyond visual prototypes into functional behavior without traditional development overhead. Designers can prototype logic, data flow, and interaction patterns that feel closer to real applications. This is especially valuable when testing assumptions about how a system responds over time, rather than how a single screen looks.

Lovable represents a newer category of tools that translate natural language intent into working applications. Designers can describe an experience, define user flows, and iteratively refine behavior through conversation. This allows designers to focus on experience orchestration rather than implementation details.

What unites these tools is not their specific features, but what they enable: the ability to prototype thinking, not just interfaces.

In an AI-enabled workflow, designers should focus early prototyping on the parts of an experience that are hardest to reason about abstractly. This often includes user flows, decision points, system responses, and moments of uncertainty.

Instead of polishing layouts too early, designers can prototype how users move through an experience, what choices they face, and how the system reacts to different inputs. These aspects are often more critical to usability and trust than visual refinement.

Conversational flows are a particularly important area for early prototyping. As AI-powered interactions become more common, designers must think carefully about how systems communicate, ask questions, handle ambiguity, and recover from errors. No-code tools make it possible to simulate these conversations and observe how users respond.

Logic and dynamic states are another priority. Many UX issues arise not from static screens, but from what happens when conditions change. Users make mistakes, data updates, systems fail, or expectations shift. Prototyping these states early helps designers identify gaps and design more resilient experiences.

Knowing what not to prototype early is just as important.

High-fidelity visuals can be useful, but they are not always necessary at the beginning. Early prototypes should focus on behavior and flow rather than polish. Fidelity should increase only as confidence increases.

Designers must learn to match fidelity to learning goals. If the goal is to understand whether users grasp a concept, rough interactions may be sufficient. If the goal is to test trust, clarity, or perceived quality, higher fidelity may be appropriate.

AI-assisted tools make it tempting to jump to polished outputs quickly. Designers must resist the urge to equate realism with readiness. A prototype that looks finished but hasn't been validated can create false confidence.

The most effective designers use no-code prototyping to learn faster, not to skip thinking.

By prototyping earlier, designers can validate assumptions before they harden into requirements. They can involve users sooner, gather more meaningful feedback, and iterate with intention. They can also communicate ideas more clearly to stakeholders and collaborators.

This approach reduces risk rather than increasing it.

No-code AI prototyping does not eliminate the need for design judgment. It amplifies it. The tools handle execution: designers handle meaning.

In the next chapters, we'll show how these tools and techniques work together in practice.

Chapter 10 – AI in the UX Design Process

Below are the common phases and activities in the User Experience (UX) design process, based on my experience as a Lead UX Designer working on global enterprise software products.

Over the years, across multiple organizations, I've seen UX teams socialize their processes in many ways. While the terminology and artifacts may vary, the fundamentals remain largely the same.

Project Kickoff

The process typically begins with a project kickoff, where the UX designer meets with the Product Manager to understand what needs to be designed. This includes defining the feature scope, business drivers, functional requirements, target users, desired business outcomes, success criteria, and release timeline.

Research Engagement

Next, the team identifies what is already known, what gaps in knowledge exist, and what research activities are needed to inform design decisions. This includes agreeing on discovery activities, usability testing, and measurement plans to assess success, customer engagement, and adoption based on the defined success criteria.

Ideation

If it is determined during kickoff that the project would benefit from a Design Sprint or ideation workshop, the team assembles a multidisciplinary group—often up to 12 participants. This group may include subject matter experts, stakeholders from Sales, Support, and Services who are close to customers, technical architects, Product Managers, Designers, and Researchers.

Best practices in user-centered design emphasize maintaining a strong focus on the user throughout the process. Bringing the *voice of the customer* into ideation workshops helps ensure that user needs, pain points, and context of use remain central to the solution being designed.

Conceptual Modeling

To ensure the solution aligns with the target user's mental model, the team creates conceptual models that describe the inputs, outputs, systems, and interactions involved in the solution. This includes identifying all actors—both human and system—and mapping high-level interactions between personas and systems.

Personas and Use Cases

The team then defines who the users are by developing personas. For each persona, the primary jobs-to-be-done are identified and documented as use cases.

Each use case is typically articulated as a user needs statement, for example:

> *"As a part-time shift worker, I need to punch in at the start of my shift so my hours worked are logged accurately on my timecard."*

A best-practice format for user needs statements is:

As <persona>, I need to <goal>, so I can <desired outcome>.

The more specific and contextual these statements are, the more effective they are at guiding design decisions.

Storyboarding

After personas and use cases are defined, the team sketches the key steps of the user journey—from initial awareness through first interaction and task completion. These storyboards often take the form of low-fidelity whiteboard or paper sketches and are reviewed and refined with user and stakeholder feedback before moving into more detailed design work.

Sketching

Designers then sketch the key screens required for the application or software. These sketches may be done on paper or digitally and are validated with users and stakeholders. Feedback from this stage is used to refine concepts before advancing to higher-fidelity designs.

Digital Wireframes

Once sketches are reviewed and refined, designers move into digital wireframing using design tools such as Figma. At this stage, wireframes may begin to reflect the company's visual brand and are typically built using an established Design Language System (DLS).

A DLS ensures consistency across products by providing pre-designed, reusable components that developers can reliably implement. In many organizations, developers can extract front-end CSS or styling information directly from Figma. DLS components are also designed to be device-agnostic, supporting responsive behavior across desktop, tablet, and mobile devices, and are crafted to meet accessibility (A11y) standards such as WCAG compliance.

Prototyping

After key views are defined, designers create interactive prototypes with just enough fidelity to gather valid usability feedback. Prototypes are often built using Figma's built-in prototyping features or tools like InVision for mobile experiences.

At this stage, the goal is learning, not perfection. Designers intentionally avoid over-polishing prototypes, so users focus on task completion, interaction flow, and usability rather than visual aesthetics. Some teams even use black-and-white or sketch-style prototypes to further reinforce this focus.

Iterative Usability Testing

Prototypes are refined through multiple rounds of usability testing. Each iteration typically includes 6–8 target users to ensure findings are actionable and reliable. Feedback from each round informs incremental design improvements.

Detailed Design Phase

Once the prototype performs well in testing and passes accessibility reviews, designers move into detailed design. This phase involves producing high-fidelity, pixel-perfect UI specifications for primary flows, alternate paths, edge cases, and error states.

This work is reviewed collaboratively with the Product–Design–Engineering triad and often goes through several rounds of refinement before final sign-off.

UI/UX Handoff

After specifications are finalized, designers conduct a handoff session with the development team. This includes walking through designs, prototypes, and interaction details, answering questions, and aligning on implementation plans.

At this point, UX also aligns with project management artifacts such as JIRA epics and stories, timelines, and expectations for ongoing design support during development.

Support During Implementation

During development, designers participate in regular sprint reviews where engineers demonstrate working builds. UX provides real-time feedback to ensure the implementation matches design intent.

Designers also support development through ad hoc communication channels such as Microsoft Teams or Slack and often maintain a shared Q&A space in tools like Confluence to support distributed teams across time zones.

Over my years as a UI/UX Designer in high tech software design, I've created many diagrams to socialize our design process.

I'm including some of the "classic UX process charts" that I've developed over the last few years, on the next few pages.

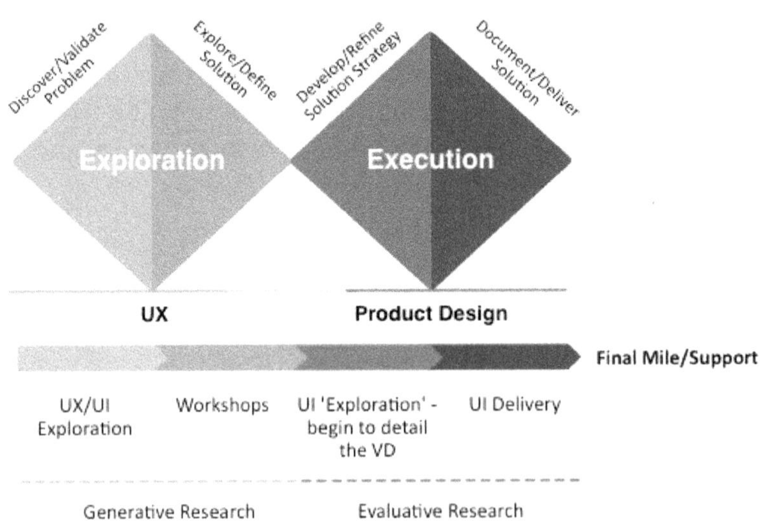

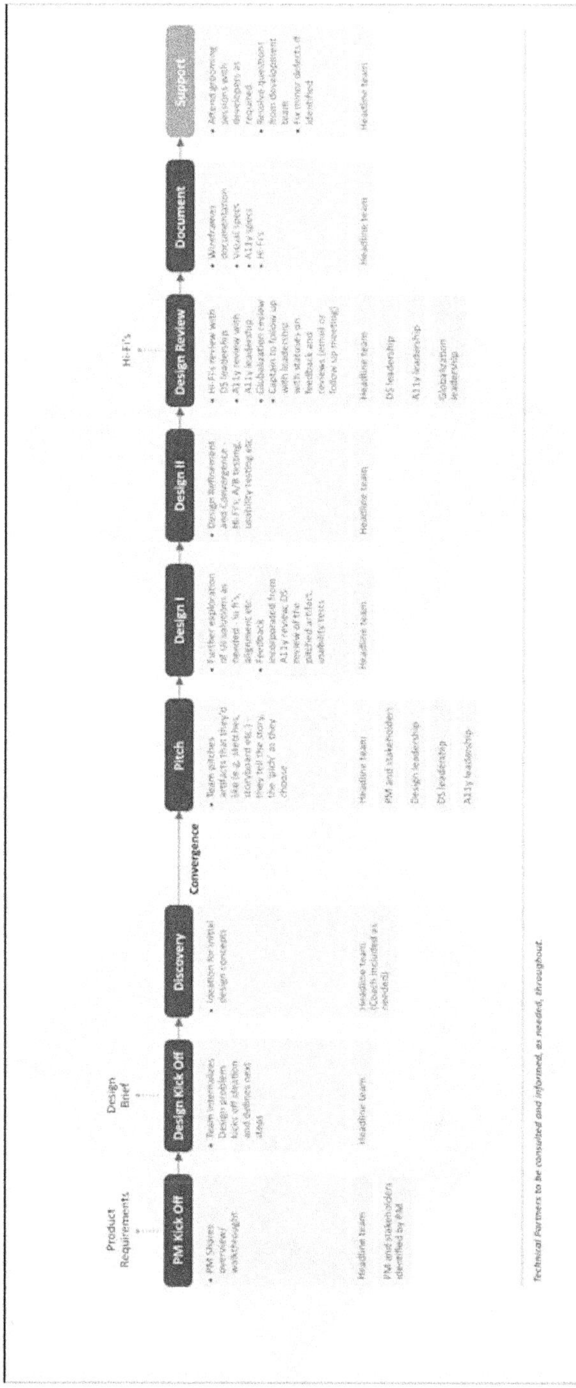
Product Requirements
Design Brief
Hi-Fi's
PM Kick Off
Design Kick Off
Discovery
Convergence
Pitch
Design I
Design II
Design Review
Document
Support
Technical Partners to be consulted and informed, as needed, throughout.

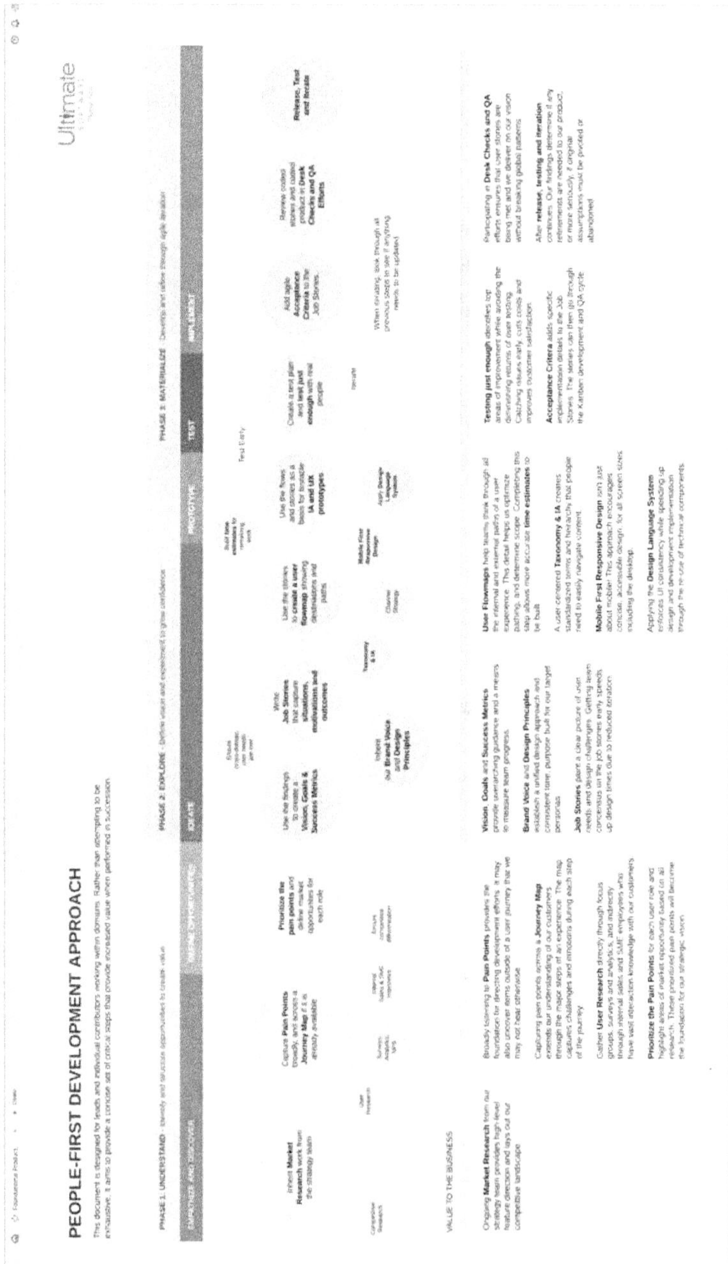
PEOPLE-FIRST DEVELOPMENT APPROACH
This document is designed for leads and individual contributors working within domains. Rather than attempting to be exhaustive, it aims to provide a concise set of critical steps that provide increased value when performed in succession.
PHASE 1: UNDERSTAND - Identify and structure opportunities to create value
PHASE 2: EXPLORE - Define vision and experiment to grow confidence
PHASE 3: MATERIALIZE - Develop and refine through agile iteration
TEST
Test Early
Inherit Market Research work from the strategy team
Capture Pain Points broadly, and across a Journey Map if it is already available
Prioritize the pain points and define market opportunities for each role
Use the findings to create a Vision, Goals & Success Metrics
Write Job Stories that capture situations, motivations and outcomes
Use the stories to create a user flowmap showing destinations and paths
Use the flows and stories as a basis for testable IA and UX prototypes
Create a test plan and test just enough with real people
Add agile Acceptance Criteria to the Job Stories
Review coded stories and coded product in Desk Checks and QA Efforts
Release, Test and Iterate
Inherit our Brand Voice and Design Principles
When iterating, look through all previous steps to see if anything needs to be updated
VALUE TO THE BUSINESS
Ongoing Market Research from our strategy team provides high-level feature direction and lays out our competitive landscape
Broadly listening to Pain Points provides the foundation for directing development efforts. It may also uncover items outside of a user journey that we may not hear otherwise
Capturing pain points across a Journey Map extends our understanding of our customers through the major steps of an experience. The map captures challenges and emotions during each step of the journey
Gather User Research directly through focus groups, surveys and analytics, and indirectly through internal sales and SME employees who have vast interaction knowledge with our customers
Prioritize the Pain Points for each user role and highlight areas of market opportunity based on all research. These prioritized pain points will become the foundation for our strategic vision
Vision, Goals and Success Metrics provide overarching guidance and a means to measure team progress
Brand Voice and Design Principles establish a unified design approach and consistent tone, purpose built for our target personas
Job Stories paint a clear picture of user needs and design challenges. Getting team concensus on the job stories early speeds up design times due to reduced iteration
User Flowmaps help teams think through all the internal and external paths of a user experience. This detail helps us optimize pathing, and determine scope. Completing this step allows more accurate time estimates to be built
A user-centered Taxonomy & IA creates standardized terms and hierarchy that people need to easily navigate content
Mobile First Responsive Design isn't just about mobile! This approach encourages concise, accessible design, for all screen sizes including the desktop
Applying the Design Language System enforces UI consistency while speeding up design and development implementation through the re-use of technical components
Testing just enough identifies top areas of improvement while avoiding the diminishing returns of over testing. Catching issues early cuts costs and improves customer satisfaction
Acceptance Critera adds specific implementation details to the Job Stories. The stories can then go through the Kanban development and QA cycle
Participating in Desk Checks and QA efforts ensures that user stories are being met and we deliver on our vision without breaking global patterns
After release, testing and iteration continues. Our findings determine if any refinements are needed to our product, or more seriously, if original assumptions must be pivoted or abandoned

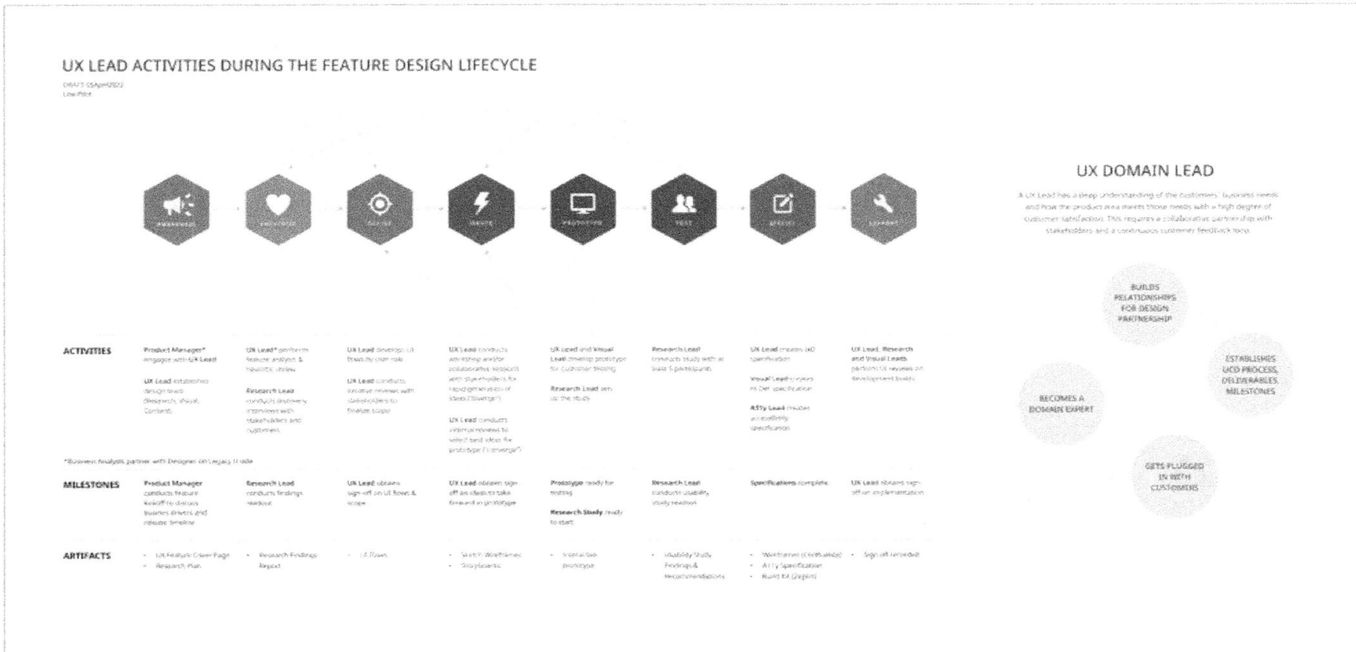
UX LEAD ACTIVITIES DURING THE FEATURE DESIGN LIFECYCLE
ACTIVITIES
MILESTONES
ARTIFACTS
UX DOMAIN LEAD
BUILDS RELATIONSHIPS FOR DESIGN PARTNERSHIP
ESTABLISHES UCD PROCESS, DELIVERABLES, MILESTONES
BECOMES A DOMAIN EXPERT
GETS PLUGGED IN WITH CUSTOMERS

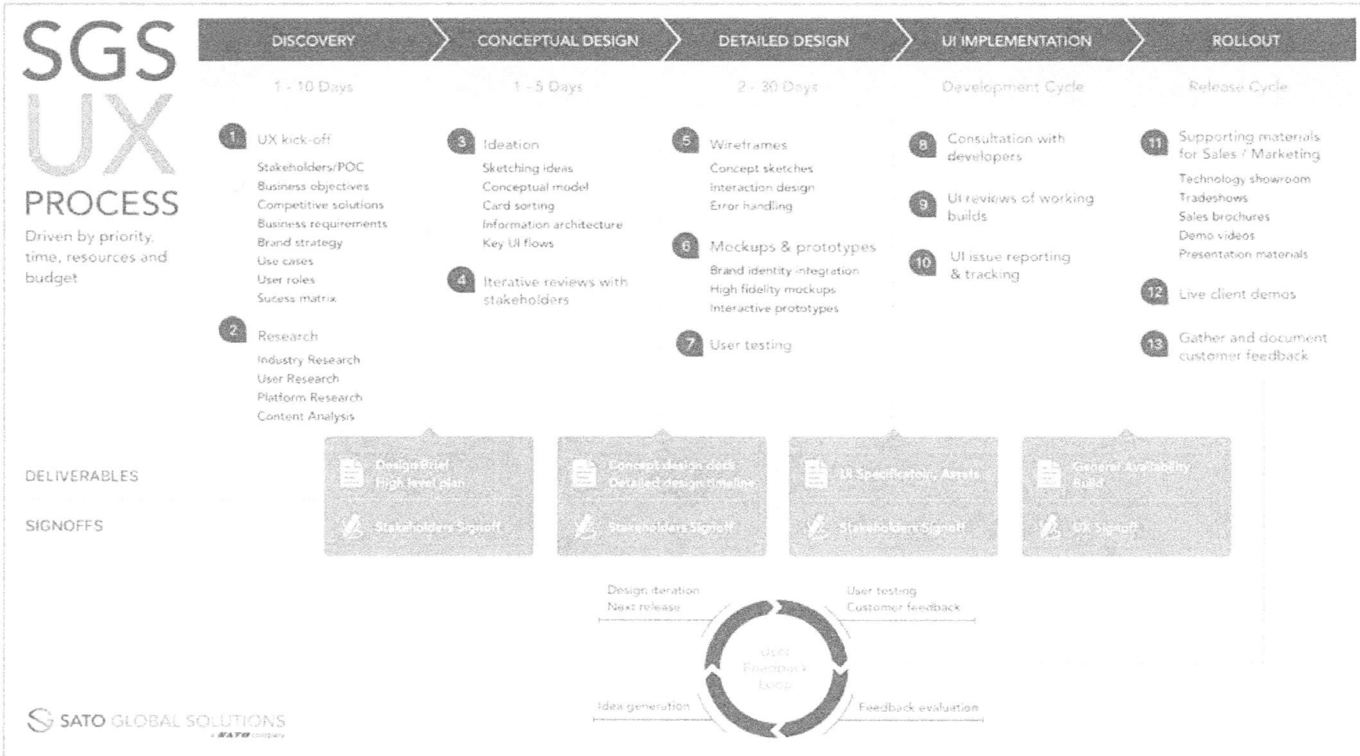
SGS
UX
PROCESS
Driven by priority, time, resources and budget
DISCOVERY
CONCEPTUAL DESIGN
DETAILED DESIGN
UI IMPLEMENTATION
ROLLOUT
1 - 10 Days
1 - 5 Days
2 - 30 Days
Development Cycle
Release Cycle
1 UX kick-off
Stakeholders/POC
Business objectives
Competitive solutions
Business requirements
Brand strategy
Use cases
User roles
Sucess matrix
2 Research
Industry Research
User Research
Platform Research
Content Analysis
3 Ideation
Sketching ideas
Conceptual model
Card sorting
Information architecture
Key UI flows
4 Iterative reviews with stakeholders
5 Wireframes
Concept sketches
Interaction design
Error handling
6 Mockups & prototypes
Brand identity integration
High fidelity mockups
Interactive prototypes
7 User testing
8 Consultation with developers
9 UI reviews of working builds
10 UI issue reporting & tracking
11 Supporting materials for Sales / Marketing
Technology showroom
Tradeshows
Sales brochures
Demo videos
Presentation materials
12 Live client demos
13 Gather and document customer feedback
DELIVERABLES
SIGNOFFS
Design Brief
High level plan
Stakeholders Signoff
Concept design docs
Detailed design timeline
Stakeholders Signoff
UI Specifications, Assets
Stakeholders Signoff
General Availability Build
UX Signoff
Design iteration
Next release
User testing
Customer feedback
Idea generation
Feedback evaluation
SATO GLOBAL SOLUTIONS

Enhancing the UX Design Process with AI

Modern AI tools don't replace the UX design process, but they **compress it, accelerate it, and reduce friction**. Designers still make the decisions, but AI dramatically shortens the time it takes to move from insight to validation.

Below is how each phase of the traditional UX process is being enhanced with AI in practice.

Project Kickoff (AI-Enhanced)

During project kickoff, I use AI tools to capture and synthesize information in real time and turn it into a structured design brief.

AI tools capture notes from the kickoff meeting and generate a clear design brief that includes:

- Overview and problem statement
- Target users and key user needs
- Design objectives
- Competitive landscape
- Business outcomes and success criteria
- Stakeholders
- Timeline and execution plan

I upload meeting recordings, transcripts, and raw notes into ChatGPT.

As an enterprise design team, we use a standardized Design Brief format. I created a custom GPT trained on that structure so it automatically organizes the content into a format I can paste directly into Confluence.

Sample Prompt — Design Brief Creation

> "You are a Senior Enterprise UX Designer.
> I am uploading a kickoff meeting transcript and raw notes.
> Please synthesize this information into a Design Brief using the following structure:
>
> - "Overview"
> - "Problem Statement"
> - "Target Users"
> - "Key User Needs"
> - "Design Objectives"
> - "Competitors"
> - "Business Outcomes"
> - "Success Criteria"
> - "Stakeholders"
> - "Timeline and Plan"
>
> Write in a clear, professional tone suitable for an enterprise Confluence page."

Write in a clear, professional tone suitable for an enterprise Confluence page."

Research Engagement (AI-Enhanced)

AI significantly reduces the time required to gather and synthesize research insights.

I use ChatGPT to:

- Identify competitors
- Analyze customer feedback from our customer community
- Summarize themes, risks, and unmet needs

I also use AI features in our research repository (such as Dovetail) to summarize insights from prior studies, allowing me to reuse existing research rather than starting from scratch.

ChatGPT helps me generate a structured research plan aligned to the project goals.

Sample Prompt — Research Synthesis

> "Summarize the key themes, pain points, and unmet needs related to [problem area] based on the uploaded customer feedback and research summaries.
>
> Organize findings into:
>
> - "Key Insights"
> - "Supporting Evidence"
> - "Opportunities for Design"
> - "Open Questions""

Sample Prompt — Research Plan

> "Create a UX research plan for a project focused on [problem statement].
>
> Include:
>
> - "Research goals"
> - "Key research questions"
> - "Target participants"
> - "Recommended methods"
> - "Success metrics"
>
> Assume an enterprise B2B software context."

Ideation (AI-Enhanced)

AI dramatically reduces the overhead required to plan and facilitate ideation.

For Design Sprint workshops, I use ChatGPT to:

- Generate a detailed daily agenda aligned with the Google 5-Day Design Sprint methodology

- Create time-boxed activities
- Draft the meeting invite and workshop description

I use Gamma to quickly generate the workshop presentation.

I use ChatGPT to:

- Generate solution ideas
- Identify key user needs and pain points
- Conduct competitive ideation research

Sample Prompt — Design Sprint Agenda

"Create a 5-day Design Sprint agenda following Google's Design Sprint methodology.

Include:

- "Daily goals"
- "Activities"
- "Time estimates"
- "Outputs for each day"

The sprint is focused on solving [problem statement] for [target users]."

Sample Prompt — Solution Ideation

"Based on the following user needs and constraints, generate multiple solution concepts.

For each concept, include:

- "Core idea"
- "User value"
- "Risks or assumptions"
- "Differentiation from competitors""

Conceptual Modeling (AI-Enhanced)

Instead of drawing conceptual models manually, I use AI to generate them quickly from natural language descriptions.

- I describe the actors, systems, and interactions conversationally.
- AI generates a conceptual diagram that I can review, refine, and validate with stakeholders.

Sample Prompt — Conceptual Model

> "Create a conceptual diagram that illustrates:
>
> - "Primary user personas"
> - "Supporting systems and services"
> - "Data inputs and outputs"
> - "High-level interactions between actors"
>
> The output should be suitable as a conceptual model for an enterprise UX review."

Personas and Use Cases (AI-Enhanced)

AI accelerates persona development and use-case synthesis.

I use ChatGPT to:

- Develop personas based on market data and research inputs
- Identify key needs, behaviors, and motivations
- Generate persona posters
- Synthesize use cases, user needs statements, and Jobs to Be Done

Sample Prompt — Persona Creation

> "Create 3 UX personas representing the primary user types for [product/domain].
>
> For each persona include:
>
> - "Role and background"
> - "Goals"
> - "Pain points"
> - "Key behaviors"
> - "Jobs to Be Done"
>
> Base this on enterprise software users."

Sample Prompt — Use Cases and User Needs

> "Based on these personas, generate:
>
> - "Top use cases"
> - "User needs statements using the format:
>   *As a [persona], I need to [goal], so I can [outcome]*""

Storyboarding (AI-Enhanced)

I still sketch storyboards by hand because it's fast and expressive—but AI removes the cleanup work.

- I sketch rough flows on a whiteboard or paper.
- I photograph the sketches and upload them to ChatGPT.
- AI redraws and digitizes them into clean storyboards or UI flow diagrams.

Sample Prompt — Storyboard Refinement

> "I am uploading a photo of a hand-drawn storyboard.
>
> Please:
>
> - "Digitize and redraw it"
> - "Preserve the intent and flow"
> - "Present it in a clean, professional format suitable for sharing with stakeholders.""

Sketching (AI-Enhanced)

- I upload rough sketches to AI tools and ask them to refine and clean up the visuals.
- The refined output is copied directly into Figma for further iteration.

Sample Prompt — Sketch Cleanup

> "Refine these rough UI sketches into clean, review-ready wireframe sketches.
>
> Maintain layout, hierarchy, and intent, but improve clarity and consistency."

Digital Wireframes (AI-Enhanced)

AI assists with several repetitive but critical tasks during wireframing:

Accessibility (AI-Enhanced)

- I upload screenshots to AI to check WCAG contrast and accessibility compliance.
- I ask AI for hex values to test contrast ratios.

Localization (AI-Enhanced)

- I upload wireframes and ask AI to generate translated strings (especially for long languages like German) to stress-test layouts.

Sample Prompt — Localization Stress Test

> "Translate all visible UI text in this wireframe into German.
>
> Optimize translations for realistic enterprise usage, not literal translation."

Placeholder Content (AI-Enhanced)

- AI generates realistic placeholder text, lists, and data patterns.

Sample Prompt – Placeholder Content

> "Generate realistic placeholder content (tables, lists, labels, and sample values) for an enterprise UX wireframe.
>
> Use domain-appropriate language, realistic data lengths, and a professional, neutral tone.
> Avoid lorem ipsum.
>
> Ensure the content is suitable for usability testing and easy to copy into Figma."

Prototyping (AI-Enhanced)

Prototyping is where AI has had the biggest impact.

What once took designers a week or more can now be done in minutes.

- Tools like Replit, Lovable, Base44, and v0.dev allow teams to generate interactive prototypes from conversational prompts.
- Designers can upload:
    - Design briefs
    - UX patterns
    - Brand guidelines
    - Screenshots of existing components

The tools generate functional prototypes that closely mimic the organization's design language system.

These prototypes can be tested with users early—*before* engineering begins—dramatically reducing risk and rework.

Why This Matters

All of these techniques allow designers to **validate ideas faster**, often saving **weeks or months** in the product lifecycle.

That means:

- Faster learning
- Better design decisions
- Reduced implementation risk
- Faster time to market
- Greater business impact

AI doesn’t replace UX designers—it removes friction so designers can focus on strategy, judgment, and human-centered problem solving.

Chapter 11 – Case Study: From Idea to Production App

Now let me walk you through a real-world example of how, as a UX designer, I was able to go from idea to interactive prototype in just a few hours—a process that previously would have taken several days or even weeks. With today's AI tools, this kind of rapid experimentation is possible in a weekend, and sometimes even in a single afternoon.

I've been experimenting with AI technology since the early versions of ChatGPT began gaining traction in late 2023. Like many people, I initially used AI for everyday personal tasks—writing, brainstorming, organizing ideas, and planning. But very quickly, I began asking a more important question: how could these tools help me do better work as a UX designer?

In my day job, I work as a Principal Designer at a global enterprise software company, a role I've held for nine years. Over time, our organization introduced locked-down, secure versions of AI tools we could use responsibly at work. That gave me the opportunity to experiment with AI in a real-world enterprise environment, where privacy, security, and trust matter.

We began using tools like ChatGPT for early thinking and drafting, Replit for prototyping, and AI embedded directly into the tools we already relied on. Copilot features appeared in Microsoft tools and collaboration workflows. AI capabilities were introduced in Figma. Even our UX research repository tools began offering AI-supported synthesis, pulling themes and actionable insights from usability sessions and helping teams learn faster from customer feedback.

At the same time, I was experimenting outside of work—partly out of curiosity, and partly because I could feel how quickly the landscape was changing. I wanted to understand what was possible when traditional timelines, handoffs, and constraints were removed.

One of the most eye-opening experiments I ran was building my UX portfolio website using a no-code tool called Lovable. The results were impressive. The site looked polished, modern, and professional, and it came together far faster than a traditional build process would have allowed. It was one of those moments that makes you stop and think, "This is real now."

Around the same time, I started following a few thought leaders who teach courses on AI tools and product building. A couple of months ago, one offering caught my attention: a weekend, two-day AI SaaS bootcamp. I assumed it would focus on prompting techniques inside popular no-code or "vibe coding" tools—tools I had already been experimenting with, including Replit and others like Bolt.new, v0.dev, and Base44.

But the bootcamp surprised me.

Instead of building through a paid platform layer, we learned how to build closer to the source. We installed

Visual Studio Code and added a Claude plugin, using Claude as a conversational interface for building an application. This approach—often referred to as Claude Code—lets you describe what you want in natural language while the system scaffolds application structure, generates code, and helps you iterate toward a deployable solution.

It completely changed how I thought about what was possible.

For years, the assumption was that building a SaaS product required a full team: a product manager to define requirements, engineers to build the system, and designers to shape the experience. SaaS—software sold as a subscription or service—traditionally meant months of planning and development.

Now, the barrier to early-stage experimentation had dropped dramatically.

This chapter documents how I applied that shift to a real product idea, using AI to support every phase of the UX process—from ideation through validated prototyping—while keeping design judgment firmly in human hands.

Case Study Overview

The idea explored in this case study is a two-sided marketplace designed to solve a growing problem in coastal communities. Boat owners often struggle to find affordable, convenient places to store their boats. At the same time, many homeowners have underutilized resources—empty docks, unused yard space, or room for trailers—and are looking for ways to offset the rising cost of living.

The opportunity was to connect these two groups through a simple, trustworthy platform.

The target users included recreational boat owners and homeowners with available storage space, particularly in high-cost waterfront areas. The business opportunity centered on facilitating short- or long-term storage arrangements that benefit both sides financially.

From the outset, there were constraints and assumptions. This was an early-stage concept. The goal was not to design a final product, but to validate whether the problem was real, the value proposition resonated, and the experience made sense to users.

Step 1: Ideation and Opportunity Framing

I began by opening a new conversation with my AI assistant and using it as a brainstorming partner. Rather than trying to fully define the product upfront, I described the idea in plain language: a web app like Airbnb, but for boat storage.

I explained the two-sided nature of the marketplace and asked a simple question: is this a viable business idea?

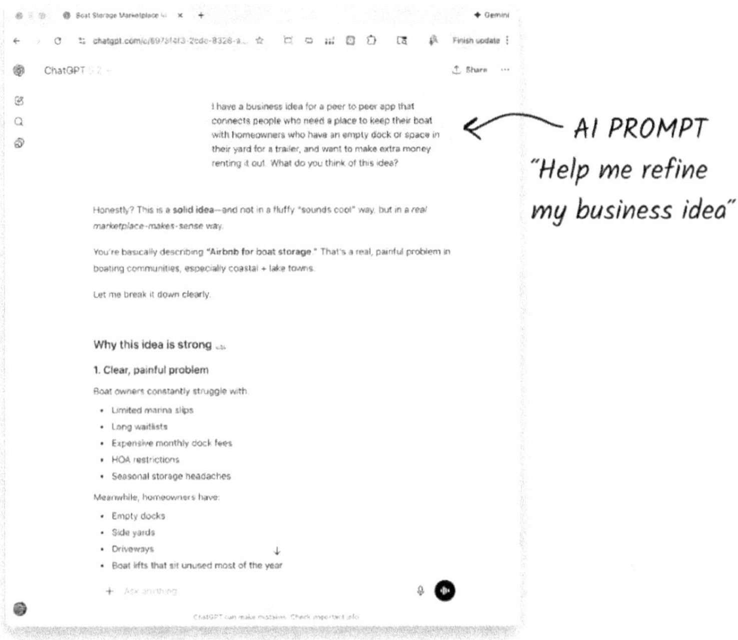

At this stage, I wasn't looking for confirmation. I wanted to surface assumptions, pressure-test the framing, and explore how the idea could be clarified. From there, I asked the AI to help summarize the concept into a concise one-page description, including a tagline, an overview, and key benefits for each user group.

I refined this output through conversation, adjusting emphasis and language until it accurately reflected what I wanted to build.

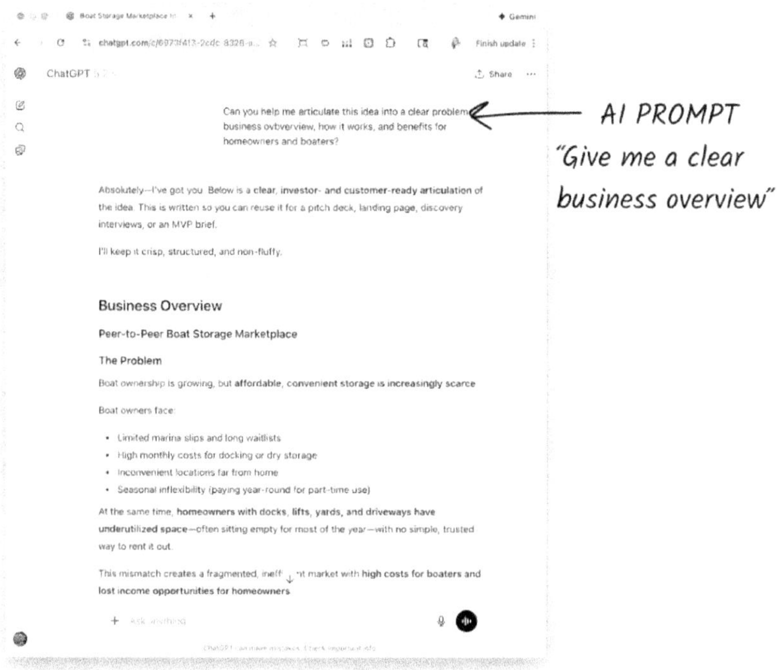

To build momentum and make the idea feel more tangible, I explored company name ideas and domain pairings that mirrored the two-sided marketplace. This wasn't about selecting a final brand—it was about making the concept feel real enough to invest in.

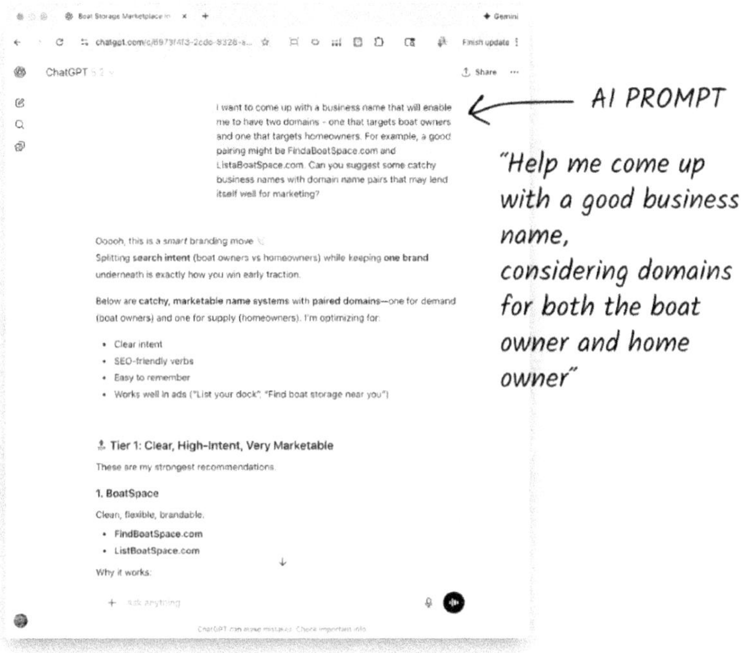

Next, I experimented with visual inspiration, generating mockups of a hypothetical vehicle wrap advertising the service. While not strictly necessary, this helped anchor the idea emotionally and reinforced that this could exist in the real world. I used an image generation AI tool to imagine what my marketing would look like on a vehicle wrap.

(Tip: Use ChatGPT to create the prompt)

Nano Banana
AI Image
Generator

AI PROMPT

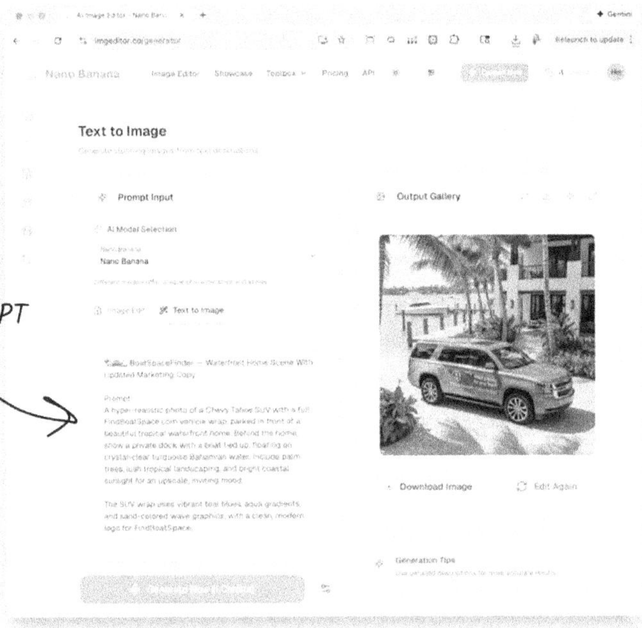

AI Generated Images
For Vision & Inspiration!

Next, I returned to fundamentals. Successful products solve real customer pain. I asked my AI assistant to articulate the problems faced by boat owners and homeowners and to describe how the service could address those needs. This sharpened the value proposition and ensured the idea wasn't just interesting, but useful.

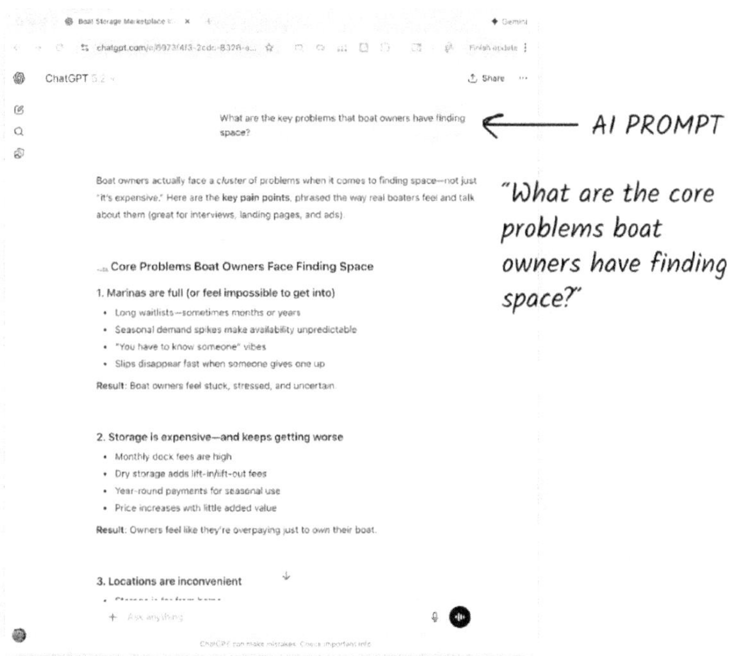

Step 2: User Needs and Personas

With the problem space clearer, I moved on to personas. I provided detailed descriptions of two representative users—one homeowner and one boat owner—and asked the AI to turn those descriptions into structured personas.

The homeowner persona represented a retired individual on a fixed income, living in a waterfront home with an unused dock and increasing financial pressure from taxes, insurance, and maintenance costs. The boat owner persona represented a couple who moved to South Florida for the boating lifestyle, only to discover how expensive and inconvenient storage could be.

The personas summarized goals, motivations, pain points, and how the service could help. Importantly, these were treated as hypotheses, not research conclusions. I asked my AI assistant to help me refine my two target personas, and this is the result.

AI Generated Persona: "Homeowner" (Host)

- *demographics*
- *goals*
- *motivations*
- *pain points*
- *opportunity*

Persona 1: The Homeowner Host

Name: Terry Williams
Age: 72
Location: Boca Raton, FL (Ocean-access canal home)
Occupation: Retired School Administrator
Living Situation: Widow, lives alone

Background

Terry has lived in her waterfront Boca Raton home for over 25 years. She and her late husband spent decades boating, entertaining friends, and enjoying life on the water. While she no longer boats herself, she still takes great pride in her home and spends much of her time gardening and enjoying the view from her backyard dock.

As a retiree on a fixed income, Terry is beginning to feel the financial pressure of rising property taxes, insurance, and maintenance costs. She wants to remain in her home for as long as possible but needs a way to make that sustainable.

Goals & Motivations

- Earn supplemental income without taking on a part-time job
- Remain financially independent
- Feel safe and secure renting her dock
- Enjoy light social interaction and feeling connected to the boating community

Pain Points

- Rising cost of living on a fixed income
- An unused dock that feels like wasted potential
- Concerns about safety, trust, and liability
- Limited technical confidence with complex apps

How ShareMyBoatSpace Helps

Terry sees an ad for ShareMyBoatSpace that promises easy, passive income from unused dock space. The ability to control who rents her dock, set availability, and communicate only through the platform makes her feel safe and empowered. As a bonus, she enjoys seeing activity on her dock again and occasionally chatting with friendly boaters who rent from her.

AI Generated Persona: "Boat Owner" (Renter)

- *demographics*
- *goals*
- *motivations*
- *pain points*
- *opportunity*

Persona 2: The Boat Owner Renter

Names: Chase & Sarah Morgan
Ages: 39 & 38
Location: Delray Beach, FL
Occupation: Chase is a Construction Project Manager, Sarah is a Marketing Consultant
Boat: 28-foot Center Console

Background

Chase and Sarah relocated to South Florida for the lifestyle—sunrise fishing trips, weekends on the water, and spontaneous boating adventures. Chase is an avid sport fisherman and regularly heads out before dawn. They recently purchased a 28-foot center console, but quickly ran into a major problem: they can't find an affordable, convenient place to keep it.

Their gated community prohibits trailers and on-property boat storage. Dry storage is expensive, requires advance scheduling, and adds stress and delays. Chase dreams of having the boat in the water and ready to go at a moment's notice—not waiting on forklifts and marina availability.

Goals & Motivations

- Keep the boat in the water and ready to use
- Avoid expensive marina and dry storage fees
- Have power for battery charging and freshwater access
- Reduce friction between life, work, and boating passion

Pain Points

- Long marina waitlists
- High monthly storage costs
- Inconvenience of dry storage scheduling
- Limited options near their home

Discovery Moment

One afternoon, stuck in traffic after work, Chase spots a sign that reads:
"Looking for a place to keep your boat?"
He pulls over, scans the QR code, and instantly browses available docks near his home on his phone. For the first time, he sees realistic, affordable options from local homeowners offering water access, power, and flexible terms.

How ShareMyBoatSpace Helps

Instead of waiting months for a marina slip, Chase and Sarah secure a nearby residential dock with power and freshwater access. Chase now launches at sunrise without delay, and Sarah enjoys stress-free weekends on the water. The platform gives them flexibility, affordability, and convenience they couldn't find anywhere else.

Next, I asked ChatGPT to generate two visual persona posters for me. This helped put a face to the customer, so I keep their needs in mind throughout the app design process.

AI Generated Persona Posters

Step 3: Business Pitch and Product Narrative

Next, I used AI to help articulate the business story. This included clarifying the value proposition, identifying points of differentiation, and defining what success would look like.

This step helped align user needs with business goals and ensured the experience wasn't being designed in isolation. It also created a narrative that could later be used to communicate the concept to partners, investors, or internal stakeholders. This is the result after refining it though a few prompts.

AI Generated Business Overview

(starting point for the AI prototyping tool)

ShareMyBoatSpace

Because every boat deserves a home.

Find local dock and yard space for your boat.

Overview

ShareMyBoatSpace is a peer-to-peer platform that connects boaters with homeowners who have extra dock, driveway, or yard space. Whether you need a short-term place to tie up or a long-term spot to store your vessel, ShareMyBoatSpace makes it easy to find — and share — local space for boats of all kinds.

How It Works

For Homeowners: List your dock, driveway, or yard space in minutes. Add photos, pricing, and availability to attract local or visiting boaters.

For Boaters: Search by location or route to find the perfect spot to dock or store your boat — on water or on land.

Book Securely: Pay safely through the platform and connect with verified, reviewed hosts in your area.

Benefits for Homeowners

Earn effortless income from unused space
Connect with your local boating community
Stay in full control — set your own pricing, terms, and availability

Benefits for Boaters

⚓ Find affordable, convenient spaces close to home or along your travels
⚓ Choose from water or land options that fit your vessel and budget
⚓ Skip the marina waitlists and high storage costs

Why It Works

ShareMyBoatSpace turns unused property into opportunity — helping homeowners earn passive income while giving boaters more flexible, affordable options to keep their boats safe, local, and cared for.

It's simple, community-driven, and built on the belief that every boat deserves a home.

Step 4: Storyboarding the Experience

Before moving into detailed design, I wanted to understand the experience as a story. I sketched a simple twelve-panel storyboard showing the end-to-end journey from discovery to successful boat storage.

I uploaded my rough sketches to my AI assistant, asking it to refine and clarify the flow. This helped translate rough ideas into a coherent experience narrative without over-investing in fidelity too early.

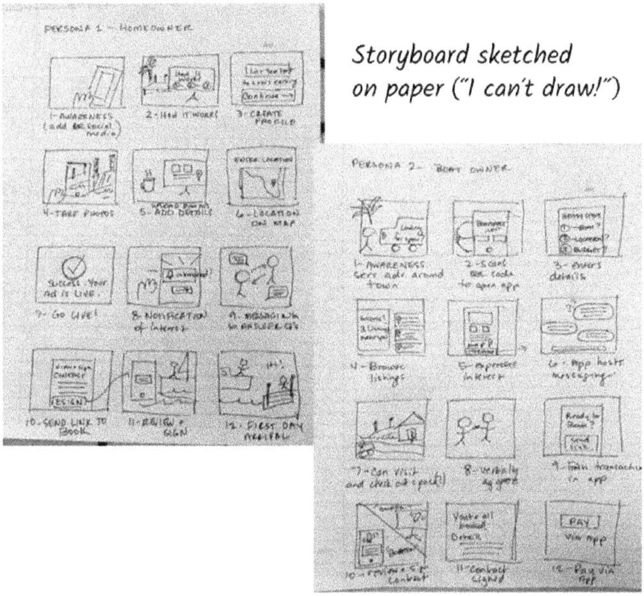

Storyboard sketched on paper ("I can't draw!")

AI Generated - from my uploaded sketches

Step 5: UI Flows and Requirements

With the story further defined, I moved into flows and requirements. I outlined happy paths and explored edge cases, thinking through how the system should behave in different scenarios.

AI helped here by surfacing gaps, identifying unclear transitions, and stress-testing assumptions. The output wasn't final requirements it was a structured starting point grounded in user needs.

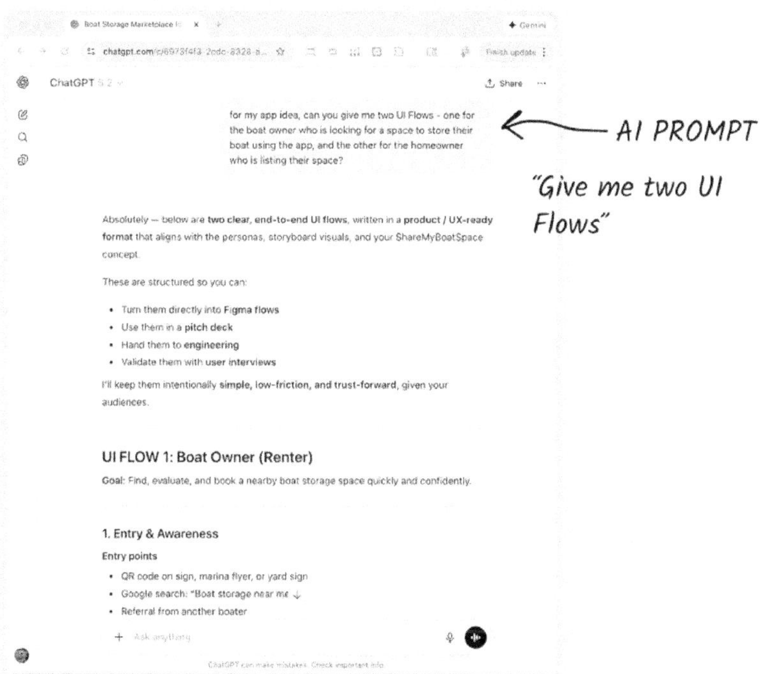

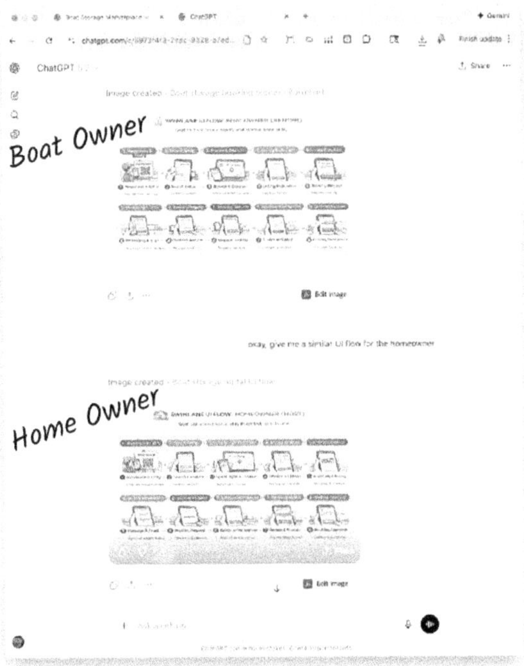

AI Generated
UI Flows for
the user journey
for each persona

SWIMLANE UI FLOW: BOAT OWNER (RENTER)

Goal: Find and book a nearby boat storage space easily

SWIMLANE UI FLOW: HOMEOWNER (HOST)

Goal: List unused space, **stay in control,** earn income

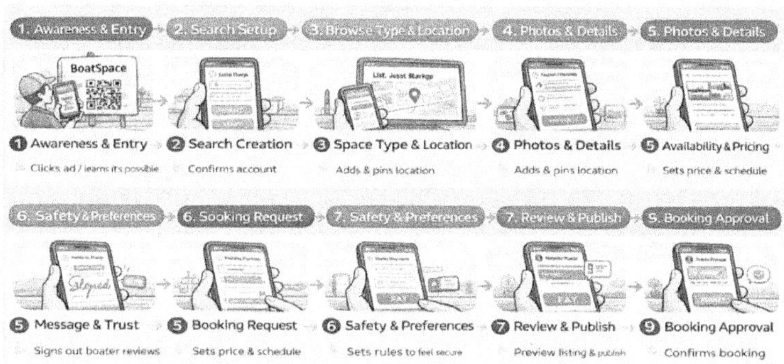

Step 6: Building the No-Code Prototype

Now that I finished the groundwork, it was time to build.

There were multiple options. I could have jumped straight into code using AI-assisted development tools. But as a UX designer, I wanted to design and validate the experience first.

I chose to build the prototype using a no-code, AI-assisted tool called Lovable that supports conversational "vibe coding." This allowed me to focus on flows, language, and behavior rather than implementation details.

As a starting point, I uploaded the refined business summary and let the tool generate an initial version of the experience. A good tip for using these tools is to find a website or app that you want to model your app after, then instruct the AI to use it as a reference.

From there, I iteratively refined the prototype through conversation—adjusting flows, clarifying copy, adding system states, and removing unnecessary complexity.

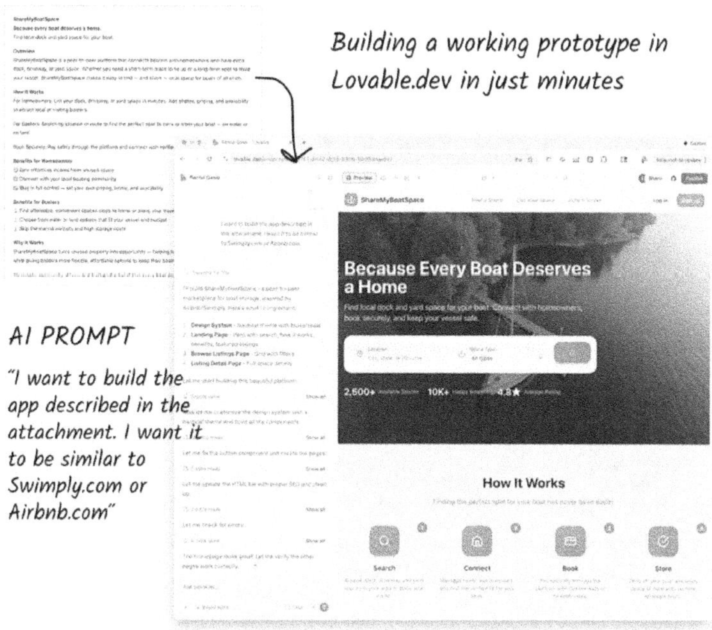

I increased fidelity only where it was needed to support meaningful usability testing. The goal wasn't polish. It was clarity.

Once the prototype reached a point where users could understand the value, complete key tasks, and express confusion where it existed, I stopped refining.

Step 7: Validation with Real Users

With a functional prototype in hand, I took it to real people. We planned to show it to boat owners, homeowners, and even a few boat yards and marinas to gauge interest and understanding.

Instead of asking abstract questions, we observed reactions. Where did users hesitate? What excited them? What concerns surfaced naturally?

Based on this feedback, I refined the prototype again—simplifying flows, clarifying expectations, and adjusting language. These changes were fast and low-risk because nothing was locked into code yet.

Only after this validation did it make sense to move forward.

Step 8: Final Prototype and Key Learnings

The final prototype represented a validated experience—not a finished product, but a confident direction. It captured what users valued, where friction existed, and how the service should behave.

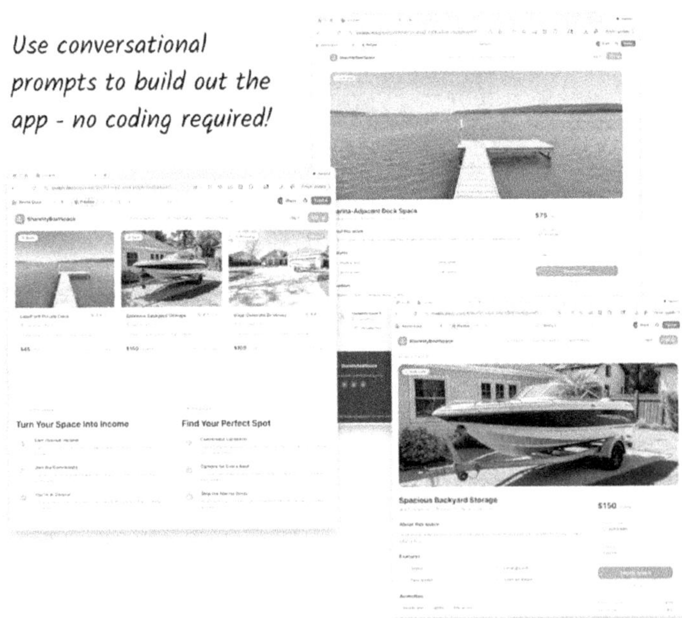

The biggest takeaway from this case study is not the specific app idea. It's the process.

AI dramatically reduced the time it took to move from idea to evidence. The tools accelerated execution, but the designer remained responsible for framing the problem, making decisions, validating with humans, and orchestrating the work.

What once required large teams and long timelines can now begin with a single designer, a clear intent, and the right tools.

Chapter 12 – From Designer to Orchestrator: AI-Assisted Software Development

For most product teams, the journey from prototype to production has traditionally been long, expensive, and fragmented. Design intent moved through handoffs, translations, and compromises before becoming real software. Even strong prototypes often lost momentum as they entered development pipelines constrained by time, resources, and competing priorities.

AI-assisted software development is changing that path.

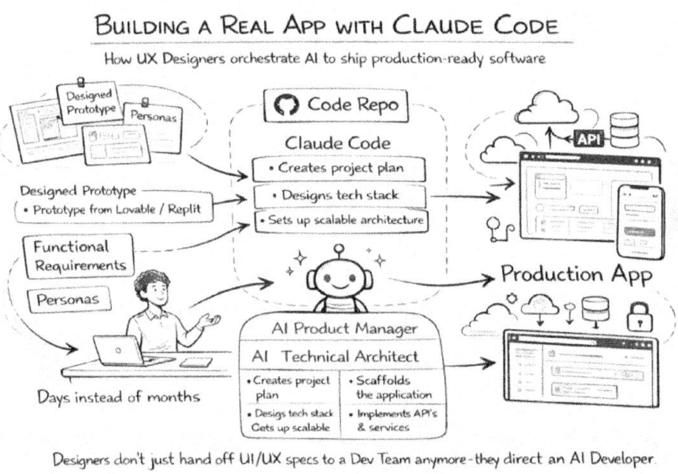

A new generation of tools now allows intent, design, and logic to flow more directly into working applications. Instead of relying on large teams and lengthy planning cycles, designers can guide AI systems that perform much of the work traditionally handled by product managers and development teams.

This shift does not eliminate the need for engineering expertise. It changes how and when that expertise is applied.

At the center of this shift are AI development assistants that operate directly inside modern development environments. One of the most impactful examples is **Claude Code**, used alongside **Visual Studio Code**. Together, they represent a new model of building software, one where intent drives implementation.

In this model, AI is not just generating snippets of code. It is participating in planning, structure, and execution.

When guided properly, AI can take on responsibilities that once required multiple roles. It can help clarify scope, break ideas into features, and reason through dependencies. It can suggest architectures, scaffold projects, define APIs, and wire services together into a coherent system. It can generate front-end and back-end structures that are not just illustrative, but deployable.

In effect, AI begins to act as both a product manager and a software development team.

As a product manager, it can help articulate goals, identify risks, and structure work. Designers can ask it to translate a validated prototype into features, user stories, and functional requirements. They can explore tradeoffs, prioritize flows, and align implementation with user intent.

As a development team, it can scaffold applications end to end. Given clear direction, AI can generate application structure, define interfaces, integrate services, and prepare a project for deployment. This dramatically reduces the gap between concept and execution.

What makes this especially powerful for designers is that the source of truth shifts.

Instead of starting from written requirements or tickets, development begins with a validated prototype. The flows, interactions, and behaviors tested with real users become the foundation of the application. Design intent is no longer interpreted downstream; it is referenced directly.

Once a prototype has been refined and validated with real users, it can be checked into **GitHub** and used as a living artifact. AI-assisted development tools can reference that prototype, along with supporting documentation, to scaffold a working application that reflects what has already been learned.

This changes the role of the designer in a fundamental way.

Designers are no longer simply preparing work for others to build. They are orchestrating systems that build. They define the vision, validate it with humans, and then guide AI to implement it responsibly.

In this role, designers must be precise. AI systems do exactly what they are instructed to do, not what designers assume they understand. Clear intent, constraints, and context matter more than ever. Ambiguity in direction leads to ambiguity in output.

This is where UX skills become essential.

Designers understand how people think, how systems should behave, and how experiences should feel. They are uniquely positioned to guide AI toward outcomes that are usable, ethical, and aligned with human needs. The better the design thinking, the better the resulting software.

This model also opens the door to entrepreneurship.

When designers can ideate, prototype, validate, and build without assembling large teams, the barrier to creating real products drops dramatically. Designers can launch internal tools, experiments, side projects, and even companies with far less overhead. They can move from idea to working application in weeks instead of years.

This does not mean every designer should become a founder. It means designers now have options.

They can lead innovation inside organizations. They can test ideas independently. They can take ownership of products in ways that were previously inaccessible.

With that power comes responsibility.

AI-generated software still requires review, testing, and ethical consideration. Security, accessibility, and long-term maintainability cannot be ignored. Designers who orchestrate AI-assisted development must know when to involve engineers, when to slow down, and when human judgment must override automation.

The future of product creation is not designer versus developer. It is designer plus AI, working in partnership with engineering expertise when it matters most.

In this future, designers are no longer waiting at the edge of the build process. They are at the center of it, guiding intent from idea to impact.

That is the shift this chapter represents.

Chapter 13 – Future-Proofing Your UX Career

The question most designers are asking today is not whether AI will change their work, but how to stay relevant as it does.

The answer is not learning every new tool, chasing trends, or trying to outpace machines at what they do best. Future-proofing a UX career means doubling down on the skills that become more valuable as automation increases, and learning how to work alongside AI in ways that amplify those strengths.

The most important skills for UX designers today are not purely technical. They are cognitive, strategic, and human.

Problem framing matters more than ever. As AI accelerates execution, the ability to define the right problem becomes a critical differentiator. Designers who can translate vague ideas into clear, testable problems will continue to lead. Those who wait for direction or focus only on outputs will struggle to stand out.

Critical thinking is equally essential. AI systems generate plausible responses quickly, but they do not evaluate impact, ethics, or context. Designers must be able to assess outputs, recognize weak reasoning, and decide when something feels right or wrong. This judgment cannot be automated.

Communication remains a core skill. Designers must articulate intent clearly to stakeholders, to users, and increasingly, to AI systems themselves. Clear thinking leads to clear prompts, clearer collaboration, and better outcomes.

Systems thinking is another key capability. As products become more interconnected and adaptive, designers must understand how components influence one another over time. This includes anticipating second-order effects, edge cases, and unintended consequences.

Empathy remains irreplaceable. While AI can simulate perspectives, it cannot truly understand human experience. Designers who invest in listening, observing, and engaging with real people will continue to uncover insights that no model can generate on its own.

These skills shape how designers should think about their portfolios.

Traditional UX portfolios often emphasize polished visuals and final deliverables. While craft still matters, future-ready portfolios focus more on thinking, process, and impact. They show how designers framed problems, navigated ambiguity, tested assumptions, and learned from failure.

For AI-related work, this becomes even more important.

Strong portfolios demonstrate how AI was used responsibly. They show where AI accelerated exploration, where human judgment guided decisions, and how outcomes were validated with real users. They make clear what the designer did versus what the tool produced.

Including artifacts like early prototypes, decision rationales, iteration points, and lessons learned helps convey maturity. Screenshots alone are no longer enough. Context matters.

Positioning yourself as an AI-first designer does not mean leading with tools. It means leading with outcomes.

AI-first designers are comfortable working with uncertainty. They know how to incorporate AI into their workflow without becoming dependent on it. They understand when speed is valuable and when slowing down leads to better decisions.

They also tend to position themselves closer to product and strategy. Rather than waiting for requirements, they help define them. Rather than handing off work, they stay involved through validation and build. This proximity increases influence and opportunity.

For some designers, this shift opens doors to leadership roles. For others, it enables entrepreneurship, consulting, or independent product creation. There is no single path forward, but there is a shared mindset: ownership.

The next generation of UX designers will grow up with AI as a given. They will not remember a time when prototyping required weeks of setup or when synthesis meant hours of manual work. Their challenge will not be access to tools but developing judgment early.

Experienced designers have a role to play here. Mentorship, critique, and modeling thoughtful practice will be essential. Teaching when not to use AI may be just as important as teaching how to use it.

UX as a discipline has always evolved alongside technology. From desktop to mobile, from static interfaces to dynamic systems, designers have adapted by focusing on people rather than platforms.

AI is simply the next evolution.

Designers who remain curious, grounded, and reflective will continue to thrive. Those who embrace AI as a partner, while maintaining responsibility for outcomes, will shape the future of products and experiences.

The tools will change. The expectations will shift. The fundamentals will endure.

The future of UX design belongs to those who understand that technology may accelerate the work, but humans still define its meaning.

Chapter 14 – Responsible AI Design Principles

Responsible AI is not a single decision or compliance step. It is a set of design principles applied repeatedly throughout the UX process. These principles help designers make intentional choices about how AI systems behave, how much power they have, and how users experience them.

The goal is not to eliminate risk entirely, but to design systems that are understandable, controllable, and aligned with human values.

The following principles translate responsible AI thinking into practical guidance for UX designers.

Human Agency and Control

AI systems should support human decision-making, not replace it.

Users should understand when AI is influencing an outcome and retain the ability to intervene, adjust, or override AI-generated results. Automation should assist progress, not remove autonomy.

Design implications include clear opt-in or opt-out mechanisms, editable AI outputs, and meaningful choices rather than forced automation.

Transparency and Explainability

Users should be able to understand what an AI system is doing at the experience level.

This does not require technical explanations of models or algorithms. It requires clarity about intent, limitations, and impact. Users should know why a suggestion is being made, what data may be influencing it, and what confidence they should place in the result.

Opaque systems erode trust. Clear systems build it.

Accountability and Ownership

AI does not take responsibility for outcomes. People and organizations do.

Designers must ensure that accountability is visible and clear. When something goes wrong, users should know who is responsible and how to seek correction or support. Responsibility should never be hidden behind automation.

UX decisions should reinforce ownership, not deflect it.

Fairness and Inclusion

AI systems can unintentionally reinforce bias or exclude certain users.

Designers must actively question whose perspectives are represented and whose are missing. This includes considering accessibility, cultural context, language, and edge cases that may not be well represented in training data.

Inclusive design practices are essential in AI systems because errors scale quickly.

Reliability and Safety

AI systems should behave consistently within defined boundaries and fail gracefully when those boundaries are exceeded.

Designers should anticipate error states, uncertainty, and misuse. When confidence is low, systems should communicate that uncertainty rather than fabricate certainty. Safety is often about knowing when not to act.

Privacy and Data Respect

AI systems often rely on user data, implicitly or explicitly.

Designers must ensure that data collection is proportionate, understandable, and respectful. Users should not be surprised by how their data is used. Consent should be meaningful, not buried.

Respect for privacy is foundational to trust.

Proportionality and Restraint

Not every experience needs AI.

Designers should ask whether AI meaningfully improves the user experience or simply adds complexity. Sometimes the most responsible design choice is a simpler, non-AI solution.

Using AI because it is possible is not the same as using it because it is valuable.

What Are the OECD AI Principles?

The **OECD AI Principles** are a set of internationally agreed guidelines for the responsible design, development, and use of artificial intelligence. They were adopted in 2019 by the Organization for Economic Co-operation and Development (OECD) and have since been endorsed by 40+ countries, including the United States, the EU, Japan, and others.

They are considered the global baseline for responsible AI and heavily influence government policy, enterprise governance, and corporate AI standards.

The OECD AI Principles define how AI systems should behave in society, not how they are technically built. They focus on **human values, trust, accountability, and safety** which is why they map so well to UX design.

There are five core principles.

1. Human-Centered Values and Fairness

AI systems should benefit people and society and respect human rights, diversity, and inclusion.

In UX terms, this means:

- Designing AI that supports user goals, not manipulates behavior.
- Avoiding experiences that disadvantage certain groups.
- Designing inclusively across abilities, cultures, and contexts.
- Treating users as people, not data points.

This principle aligns directly with human-centered design.

2. Transparency and Explainability

People should be able to understand when AI is being used and how it affects outcomes.

In UX terms, this means:

- Making AI involvement visible in the experience.
- Explaining AI behavior in human language, not technical jargon.
- Helping users understand *why* a suggestion or decision was made.
- Avoiding "black box" experiences where outcomes feel mysterious.

This is about clarity, not technical disclosure.

3. Robustness, Security, and Safety

AI systems should function reliably and safely across expected and unexpected situations.

In UX terms, this means:

- Designing for edge cases and failure states.
- Communicating uncertainty instead of fabricating confidence.
- Handling errors gracefully.
- Preventing harmful or unsafe interactions.

Good UX is often the difference between a safe system and a dangerous one.

4. Accountability

Organizations and individuals should be accountable for AI outcomes.

In UX terms, this means:

- Making responsibility visible, not hidden behind automation.
- Giving users clear paths to report issues or correct errors.
- Avoiding language that implies "the system decided" without recourse.

AI should never appear to be an untouchable authority.

5. Human Oversight and Control

Humans should be able to intervene or override AI systems when necessary.

In UX terms, this means:

- Designing for human override.
- Allowing users to edit, reject, or undo AI outputs.
- Avoiding forced automation.
- Preserving user agency at critical decision points.

This is one of the most important UX responsibilities in AI systems.

Why OECD AI Principles Matter for UX Designers

Even though the OECD AI Principles are often discussed at a policy or executive level, they are implemented through UX decisions.

UX designers operationalize these principles by:

- What users see.
- What choices users have.
- How systems communicate confidence or uncertainty.
- How control is shared between humans and AI.

If you design the experience, you are implementing the OECD AI Principles, whether you realize it or not.

Glossary

Artificial Intelligence (AI)
A broad category of systems designed to perform tasks that typically require human intelligence, such as learning, reasoning, and decision-making.

Generative AI
A class of AI systems that create new content—such as text, images, designs, or code—based on patterns learned from data rather than retrieving predefined answers.

Large Language Model (LLM)
An AI system trained on large amounts of text data to generate and understand language by predicting what comes next based on context.

Prompt
An input provided to a generative AI system that sets context, intent, and constraints for the output.

Prompting
The practice of guiding AI systems through iterative instructions and context, like framing design problems or research questions.

Proto-Persona
An early, assumption-based representation of a user created to align teams and guide research planning, not to replace real user data.

Jobs to Be Done (JTBD)
A framework that focuses on what users are trying to accomplish rather than who they are, emphasizing progress over demographics.

Shift-Left Prototyping
The practice of creating and testing prototypes earlier in the UX process to surface learning sooner and reduce downstream risk.

No-Code Tools
Platforms that allow users to build functional software using visual interfaces or natural language instead of traditional programming.

AI-Assisted Development
A workflow in which AI systems help plan, scaffold, or generate software based on human-defined intent and constraints.

Human-in-the-Loop
A design approach that ensures humans retain oversight, judgment, and control within AI-supported systems.

Hallucination
When an AI system generates output that appears plausible but is incorrect, fabricated, or unsupported by evidence.

References and Further Reading

The following resources are trusted starting points for UX designers who want to learn how to work with artificial intelligence responsibly, effectively, and with a human-centered mindset. These references focus on practical application, ethical considerations, and ongoing learning rather than technical implementation.

General AI Literacy for Designers

OpenAI — ChatGPT Guides and Documentation
https://platform.openai.com/docs

Anthropic — Claude Usage and AI Safety Principles
https://www.anthropic.com

Google — Gemini and Responsible AI Resources
https://ai.google/responsibility

UX and Human-Centered AI

Nielsen Norman Group — AI and UX Research
https://www.nngroup.com

IDEO — Human-Centered AI Thinking
https://www.ideo.com

ACM (Association for Computing Machinery) — Human-Centered AI Research
https://www.acm.org

Design and Prototyping Tools

Figma — AI Features and UX Workflows
https://www.figma.com

Replit — AI-Assisted Prototyping
https://replit.com

Lovable — Prompt-to-App Prototyping
https://lovable.dev

Responsible and Ethical AI

Partnership on AI
https://partnershiponai.org

Organisation for Economic Co-operation and Development (OECD) — AI Principles
https://oecd.ai

Stanford Human-Centered AI Institute (HAI)
https://hai.stanford.edu

Learning and Community

UX Collective
https://uxdesign.cc

Interaction Design Foundation
https://www.interaction-design.org

www.ingramcontent.com/pod-product-compliance
Lightning Source LLC
LaVergne TN
LVHW022229200926
848481LV00006B/2195

* 9 7 8 1 8 0 7 7 8 7 5 9 2 *